*a Consumer Publication*

WILLS
AND
PROBATE

Consumers' Association
publishers of **Which?**
14 Buckingham Street
London WC2N 6DS

a Consumer Publication

*edited by* Edith Rudinger

*published by* Consumers' Association
publishers of **Which?**

Consumer Publications are
available from Consumers'
Association and from
booksellers. Details of
other Consumer Publications
are given at the end of
this book.

ISBN 0 85202 098 8

Second edition December 1967
Third edition September 1969
Fourth edition May 1970
Fifth edition September 1972
Amended reprint June 1973
April 1975

Computer set and printed in
England by Page Bros (Norwich)
Ltd, Norwich

# CONTENTS

Note, April 1975
Foreword
Making a will                      *page*      1
— in Scotland                                 44
Probate                                       48
Administration in Scotland                   140
Distribution on intestacy                    145
— in Scotland                                155
Index                                        157

# NOTE TO APRIL 1975 EDITION, FOLLOWING THE INTRODUCTION OF CAPITAL TRANSFER TAX.

See mainly pages 9, 10, 102, 106–110

The property of someone who has died after 12 March 1975 is liable to capital transfer tax (CTT), instead of estate duty. The procedure for paying capital transfer tax on death is much the same as it was for paying the now repealed estate duty. The executors or administrators have to prepare the same forms as in the past and many of the rules are the same, especially in matters of detail. The forms will gradually be replaced by new ones. In the meantime, any reference to estate duty on the forms, is to be taken as referring to CTT. Capital transfer tax is administered by the Estate Duty Office, which has not had its name changed.

The most important difference between capital transfer tax on death and estate duty is that the new tax takes into account taxable gifts made during a person's life (not just those within seven years of death—see page 102) as well as the property he leaves when he dies. Gifts made after 26 March 1974 are counted, and the tax is calculated on the total of the taxable lifetime gifts and of the estate left on death. This affects the rate of tax payable on death, because the more a person gave away during his life, the higher the rate payable on his death (pages 59, 106–110).

Gifts to your wife or husband are exempt from

CTT, both in life and on death (so the point on page 16 about avoiding paying duty twice where husband and wife may die together, or soon after each other, is no longer valid).

CTT on most assets has to be paid when applying for probate, just as estate duty had to be (pages 87–89). So it is still necessary as a rule to borrow money to pay the tax, until the assets of the estate can be made available to the personal representatives (see page 87—that procedure still applies). For CTT, it is not any longer essential for the executors to swear an affidavit about the value of the estate: signing is now sufficient (pages 94, 111). But for the probate itself it is still necessary to swear an oath.

Interest is payable on all CTT on death from the end of the sixth month after death and is 6 per cent, not 3 per cent (compare page 107). Houses, buildings and land are liable for interest now, just like other property. Payment by instalments over eight years is still possible for houses, land, buildings and some un-quoted shares (page 107), but becomes immediately due if the property is sold.

The basis of charging CTT for the estates of people who died after 12 March 1975 is as follows. Assuming there were no taxable gifts in the decea-sed's lifetime (and some lifetime gifts are not taxable, for example, gifts amounting to less than a total of £1,000 in any one year), the first £15,000 of the net estate is exempt from tax, that is, you only pay tax on any excess over £15,000. All property left to the widow or widower is also exempt. In Herbert Blake's case, therefore, only £2,000 (the sum left to his chil-dren) would come into the calculation for CTT, and as that amounts to less than £15,000 no tax would be payable (compare page 109). But on Mrs Blake's death, assuming she did not marry again, duty would be payable on everything she leaves over £15,000.

The rates of CTT payable on a death are calculated in slices.

Nothing below £15,000;

Between £15,000 and £20,000 the rate is 10 per cent;

From £20,000 to £25,000 the rate is 15 per cent;

£25,000 to £30,000 it is 20 per cent;

£30,000 to £40,000 it is 25 per cent;

£40,000 to £50,000 it is 30 per cent;

£50,000 to £60,000 it is 35 per cent;

£60,000 to £80,000 it is 40 per cent;

£80,000 to £100,000 it is 45 per cent;

The top rate (on estates over £2 million) is 75 per cent.

As with estate duty, it may be necessary to correct values, or to add or subtract items, as a result of matters coming to light after originally applying for grant of probate. It is no longer necessary for corrective accounts to be sworn (see page 111). A clearance certificate should still be sought (see page 118).

Death, it has been said, is the new taboo, the subject people do not think about. Making a will has therefore lost some of the appeal it used to have, and many people defer, until it is too late, deciding what is to happen to their possessions when they die.

This book is intended to help at two separate stages, which in any individual case should be separated by a decent interval.

Firstly, it explains how to make a will in a simple case, including a description of what not to do, what to include and how the will must be signed and witnessed. Secondly, the book describes the administration by the executors of the estate of someone who has died. Here, too, only the straight forward case is described, but this is done in some detail, to give the full picture. What happens when there is no will is also explained.

The probate registry provides special machinery to deal with laymen who wish to act as personal representatives without having a solicitor. This book supplements this by explaining, in detail, not only the probate registry procedure but also what goes before and what comes after. Nevertheless, there will always be a great number of cases where a solicitor is essential.

This book explains the law and procedure in England and Wales; the main differences which operate in Scotland appear at the end of each chapter. This book does not cover what happens in Northern Ireland.

Some people have an unconscious fear of making a will, as if to do so were to take a positive step towards the grave. Others, when asked if they have made a will, smile nervously and say that they have so little to leave that it would not be worth the trouble. But the total value of a person's property is not much of a factor in considering this. A man might have only £250, but his circumstances could make it essential that he should leave a will, to prevent his property going to the crown. His neighbour might have £100,000 and yet not have to make a will at all in order to fulfil his wishes.

*Intestacy*

The property of a person who dies without leaving a valid will—dying intestate, the law calls it—is divided among his family according to rules in the Administration of Estates Act, which applies to anyone whose domicile, that is his permanent home, at the time of his death is in England or Wales, even if he died elsewhere. Where his possessions are worth under £15,000 all will go to his widow. Where it is more than that, the position becomes more complicated. The widow gets the furniture, the car and the rest of the personal effects of her late husband, together with the first £15,000 out of the stocks, shares, insurance policies, bank accounts, the house and so on. What is then left is divided into two halves. One half goes to the children equally, there and then. As to the other half, the widow gets a life interest in it: an income consisting of dividends from shares, rent from houses, and so on, for the rest of her life. On her death, the property comprising the half share from which she has been receiving the income is then divided equally among the children, just as the first half was earlier on. If no wife survives, the whole estate is divided between the children equally. If there is a wife, but no children, she gets everything up to £40,000 and half the rest. The other half of the rest goes to the parents of the man who died.

On a wife's death intestate her property is divided in the same way as a husband's.

The property of a bachelor who dies intestate is divided between his parents; if they are dead, his brothers and sisters share it; if he has none, his grandparents share it; and if they are dead, aunts and uncles share the estate. The children of an eligible relative who has already died generally receive the share which their parent would have received. If a bachelor dies without any descendants of his grandparents alive to inherit his property, his estate goes to the crown, if he has made no will.

On a spinster's death intestate, her property is divided in the same way as a bachelor's.

None of the property of a man or woman who is divorced goes to the ex-spouse, under the intestacy rules.

These are the intestacy rules in outline. They are described in greater detail at the end of this book. If you wish your property to be divided according to the rules just described, there is no pressing need for you to make a will, as your wishes will probably be met by the automatic operation of the intestacy rules.

But there are advantages in making a will, even so. Firstly, you may become better off as the years go by, and while the intestacy rules may suit your present financial position, they may not be appropriate in a few years' time.

Next, you have to take account of inflation and the fall in the value of money. If your property, excluding the personal effects, comes to more than £15,000 so that your widow will get a life interest, she may be all right at first, according to current values and rates of interest. But she may survive you for many years, and she may find that what was at first a perfectly adequate income for her to live on has depreciated to a pittance.

Where there is an intestacy, there are restrictions on what sort of investments can be used for the widow's life interest (she cannot touch the capital, of course, apart from the first £15,000, as she is only entitled to the income). But if you make a will you can remove these restrictions and so give her a chance to have a better income.

You may also have to consider the possibility of a husband and wife being killed together in an accident, leaving young children behind. Were this to happen, the property of both would be held on trust till the children came of age. In the meantime it would have to be invested, and the restrictions on the kind of investments that can be selected may prevent the property being dealt with as flexibly and advantageously for the benefit of the children as might have been wished. Making a will could give greater freedom regarding investments, and the children could be better off.

If you have left no will, the nearest relatives are the ones primarily entitled to take on the legal side of managing your estate (that is the property you leave behind)—to be what are called the administrators. If you make a will, however, you can choose who shall take on this task. In this case, those appointed to act are called executors. If, therefore, your preference is to have someone who is a near relative to administer your estate—a friend, say, or your solicitor—you need to make a will.

All in all, therefore, it is better to make a will, even if the intestacy rules would dispose of your property as you would wish.

### Do-it-yourself?

There is one thing worse than not making a will at all: making a mess of making a will. Lawyers say that they make more money out of home-made wills than they do out of drawing up wills for clients.

There is probably some truth in this. Many people who prepare and sign their own will go wrong in one or more ways, with the result that after their death there could be long and expensive court cases to get the trouble sorted out. A will is a technical legal document. Problems can easily arise about whether it was signed and witnessed properly and about the exact meaning of what it says. It is not surprising, therefore, that laymen sometimes go astray when they embark on will-making unaided.

There is no legal requirement that a will should be drawn up or witnessed by a solicitor and quite a lot of people do in fact make their own. You can buy a printed form in a stationer's shop, and make your will by filling in the blanks and signing according to the directions. This is not a good idea. The form may be misleading, and by striving to make the wording of your will fit the framework of the form, you may easily find that you have inadvertently committed some blunder. It is better to avoid forms altogether, and instead to write the whole thing out from scratch.

A solicitor is likely to charge anything from five to fifty pounds for preparing a will in a normal case, depending on the circumstances. Sometimes a solicitor is essential. If, for example, a person is enjoying an income from a family trust during his lifetime, and has the right, under the trust, to determine by his will who should benefit from the trust property on his death, the will by which he does this should obviously be prepared by a solicitor, because technical legal language is needed to deal with the matter properly. Again, if the permanent home of a person making a will is in a foreign country, or some other foreign element is involved, a solicitor should be consulted.

No matter how simple the circumstances, a larger estate is more likely to benefit from legal advice, especially when it comes to questions of tax planning and saving estate duty. Smaller estates can also benefit from good advice. But the smaller your estate is going to be, the less likely it is that there is scope for sidestepping the Inland Revenue.

A solicitor should also be consulted where your assets include a business or a farm, shares in a family private company, or items of a peculiar character; likewise, where you are separated, but not divorced, from your wife or husband, and in any case where you intend to cut your spouse or your children out of your will.   It is only, in fact, where your affairs are straightforward that you should contemplate making a will without going to a solicitor. Anything unusual in your financial or family situation should be regarded as a reason for not making a will by yourself.

*Formalities.*

You must be of age, that is at least 18, to make a will. The legal formalities for making a will apply to any person whose permanent home is in England or Wales. Scottish law about wills is somewhat different. The situation in Northern Ireland is nearly the same as in England and Wales.

The most important part of your will is obviously the part which states how you wish your property to be divided when you die. Before you start writing the will itself, you should have given careful consideration to this. Jot down on a piece of paper what you think you are worth, all told. Knock off your debts, including mortgages. Consider what changes are likely to take place in your total wealth in the next five years or so, and take those changes into account in estimating your wealth. Make a list of all the people whom you might wish to benefit. Then you can decide how to divide up your property. You may want to leave specific items of property to some people: your wedding ring to your granddaughter, for example, or the piano to your musical nephew. Then you may wish to give money to a few of your relations and friends: £100 to the child of an old friend, or £25 to the boy next door. You may wish to leave the same sum to each of a number of your relations: '£200 to each of my brothers and sisters living at my death' would be suitable. Or you could, if you like, divide a larger sum between a class of relations: '£1,000 to be divided equally between all my grand-children living at my death'. But there are some dangers in describing people in your will as a class, rather than naming them individually. Does the word children include adopted and illegitimate children, for instance? Are a husband's brother's sons covered by the word nephews? Are the husbands of aunts inclu-ded in the word uncles, or does it mean brothers of parents only? To avoid any difficulties of that kind, it is better to list them all with their names.

Some people wish to leave money to a charity, and there is generally no problem about this. It is usually sufficient to say: 'I give £200 to the Imperial Cancer Research Fund'. Sometimes these words are added: '. . . and the receipt of the secretary or treasurer for the time being shall be a sufficient discharge to my executors', but they are not really necessary. It is a good idea to get in touch with the charity and find out what is its official title. Is Oxfam the right name to use in a will, for instance? Is it sufficient just to write 'Dr Barnaddo's'? A charity will probably be glad to be asked about this, because getting its name right in your will may make the difference between it getting the money or not, when the time comes. While in contact with them on this point, you should ask them whether they want to suggest any particular form of words in a will under which they are to receive a legacy. If they do, you may as well adopt the clause they suggest.

Then you have to decide who is to inherit the rest of your property. It is not practical to give away everything in stated bits so as to dispose of the lot of it exactly. Even if you could make the necessary calculation in relation to your current wealth—'£150 to cousin George, and £3,427·68 to my brother Sidney' for instance—it would not apply next month, when you will be that much richer or poorer, and certainly not next year, or the year after. So what you do is this: after disposing of specified items and sums of money, you give the remainder—the residue, lawyers call it—to some named person, who thus inherits the residue of your estate, whatever it turns out to be. You could, of course, provide that your residue should be divided, in whatever proportions you like, among a number of people. Furthermore, you could provide that the residue should be invested, and only the income paid to someone (your wife, perhaps) during her life, the money itself to be divided between other people (your children, perhaps) on the death of the life tenant (the person entitled to the income for life).

*how you dispose of your property is up to you*

How you dispose of your property is up to you, but there are several points you should consider. Most people naturally favour the members of their own immediate family, and this is a notion which the law encourages, for you are not entirely free to dispose of your property as you like. If for any reason you decide that your wife, husband, or any of your children should inherit little or nothing under your will, any of them might apply to the executors, or to the court, after your death, for reasonable provision to be made for them out of what you left. This has only been possible since 1939. Before that, a man could, for example, bequeath all his riches to his mistress or to a charity, leaving his widow destitute, but this is not so now. Those who can apply for some provision to be made are: the surviving husband or wife; sons who are under age or, if older, who are incapable of maintaining themselves; and daughters who are not married or who, if married, are incapable of maintaining themselves. Any idea you may have of disinheriting a spouse or child is therefore liable to be frustrated.

When considering giving specific items in your will, remember that a will speaks from death, that is, it will apply to your personal situation at the time of your death, not at the time you make the will. If, for example, after making a will but before you die, you sell the item of jewellery you left to your god-daughter, she will get nothing. Because of this, you may wish to provide that, if this should happen, another item should be substituted for it.

Estate duty, the only current form of death duty, depends on the total value of the estate, and not on the relationship of the beneficiaries to the deceased. Duty on property other than land and buildings is generally paid out of the residue, so that the beneficiaries who receive stocks and shares, or sums of money, get their inheritance in full. But in the case of houses and land, the beneficiary normally bears an appropriate proportion of the duty. The will can, however, specifically provide that the estate duty even on a house should be paid out of the residue. This is done by saying, for example, 'I leave my house, 22 Pridham Place, to my nephew Fred Redhill, free of duty'.

In most cases it is not necessary in making a will to calculate by how much the residue will be reduced by estate duty, funeral expenses and legal costs, because the residue will constitute the great bulk of your estate anyway. If your estate will be greatly depleted by the gifts of individual items (the specific bequests) and the gifts of stated sums of money (the pecuniary legacies), you have to remember that it is, in effect, the residuary legatee who generally has to pay the estate duty, the funeral expenses and the legal costs of administration.

*Executors*

Before you can start to write the will itself, you must decide who are to be your executors. It is by no means a mere formality to be an executor: there can be a good deal of work and a great deal of responsibility involved in this task. It would be unfair to inflict this job on someone who would have preferred not to have been appointed. A person cannot be compelled to act as an executor if he really does not want to, but it can happen that a person feels he ought to accept, having been appointed, even though he would have declined if given the chance when the will was being drawn up. So it is important to find out in advance whether a person you have in mind to be your executor is willing to be appointed. If he is not, appoint somebody else.

Whom should you appoint? In normal circumstances, a husband will appoint his wife to be an executor, and vice versa, especially where they do not have grown-up children. This is a good idea as a rule, because the wife is probably the residuary legatee. It is sensible that the person who has the biggest stake in the estate should have a hand in its administration. It is perhaps as well, though, that a wife should not have to shoulder this burden alone. She will have enough to cope with at the time of her husband's death without this, so it is often a good idea to appoint another executor to act with her. A grown-up son or daughter would be an obvious choice. If you have grown-up children, you may prefer to appoint them without appointing your wife, if only to transfer the work and responsibility into their hands.

A close friend of the family is sometimes a suitable choice for co-executor with the surviving spouse, or perhaps a near relation who is used to dealing with business affairs. When someone not in the immediate family circle is appointed as executor, it is sometimes thought suitable to leave him a legacy—£100 say— for undertaking the office of executor.

It is common to appoint a solicitor to be an executor; in this case it is important that the solicitor should prepare the will. If he does, he will include a clause in your will enabling him to charge normal professional fees for his legal work in administering the estate. Without a charging clause, as it is called, he would not be entitled to a fee. His charge for preparing the will may be nominal, only two or three pounds. He knows that he will have the advantage of dealing with the legal side of administering the estate in due course.

A bank can act as the executor of your will, and quite a lot of people appoint a bank to do this job. There are certainly situations where a bank is the most suitable choice. One is where there is family strife to such an extent that any executor appointed from within the family is likely to cause discontent. Also, a bank may be the best choice where the main beneficiary cannot be the executor for some reason, and there is no other suitable individual at hand; this could happen, for instance, where a widow is making a will in favour of her young children. An advantage of appointing a bank is that it can claim to be experienced in questions of investment and of trust management generally, and this might be useful. A bank can be a good choice where the will creates trusts which are likely to continue for many years; for example, a trust giving your widow the income from your estate for the rest of her life—a life interest, in fact. Here, one advantage of having a bank is that it goes on for ever, whereas mortal trustees will need replacement sooner or later, which can be a bother and an expense.

Like all promotional material issued by commercial organisations, the bank's literature about executorship should be looked at carefully to see what it omits. It is unlikely to point out the disadvantages.

The main reason why people do not appoint a bank to be their executor is the cost. Banks do not work for nothing, and require to be paid for acting as executors. This is often a percentage of the net value of the estate itself, plus a percentage of the annual income, where a continuing trust is created by the will. On top of this, solicitors' fees for the probate work are likely to be charged.

All in all it is probably better to appoint individuals to be your executors, if suitable candidates are willing to act. There are likely to be at least some tasks which fall on them requiring a personal touch: arranging the funeral, for instance. Banks may employ competent and sympathetic staff, but they are no substitute for the right friend or relation.

The Public Trustee is a government department which can be appointed to be your executor, as can some trust corporations. These all operate in much the same way as a bank acting as executor, and charge for providing this service. (National Giro, the post office money transfer banking service, cannot act as executor for its customers.)

A final advantage of appointing a bank as your executor is that you can be pretty sure that it will survive you, no matter how long you live, whereas there is always some chance that an executor you appoint will die before you. For the same reason it is better to select younger rather than older people to be your executors. Even so, it is best to provide in your will for a substitute executor to act in case one or other of those appointed should predecease you.

If you appoint a bank to be your executor, do so by adopting the clause which the particular bank suggests for the purpose. The local bank manager can supply you with a copy and may ask to see a draft of the will.

*Beneficiary dying first*
If a child of yours, destined to receive something under your will, were to die before you, his family would usually get that child's share. Anyone else destined to receive something under your will who dies before you will not inherit from you. In the case of an ordinary legacy ('£100 to John Brown') or a specific bequest ('my diamond brooch to Jane Brown') no problem arises, as the item will simply fall into residue, that is, swell the amount that will go to the person who is to receive the residue. What if the residuary legatee himself dies first? In that event, you would leave part of your property undisposed of; this is called a partial intestacy. For example, the average husband gives the main part of his estate to his wife, so that the wife becomes the residuary legatee. But what if the wife were to die first? It is true that then the husband could make a fresh will, making provision for the children instead, or, if there are no children, disposing of it elsewhere according to the circumstance. But it might happen that husband and wife are both victims of the same road accident, the wife being killed outright and the husband surviving for a few days, but then dying without having a chance to make a new will. In such a case, the hus-

band's will, leaving everything to his wife, would be largely abortive, because she would have died first.

What then would happen to the bulk of his property, which his will left her, depends on the rules about intestacy. These might well not accord with his wishes, so that it would be better for the husband to make specific provision for this possibility in the will itself, by saying who will take his property if his wife does not survive him. In many cases, this would be the children. If they are under age, the will might well go on to deal with that situation in greater detail. It is often felt necessary to lift some of the restrictions which would otherwise limit the executors' powers of investing the property for the children's benefit, and similar matters. The executors might feel a bit hampered in running the trust which would arise for the children until they come of age, unless the will gave them a free hand to do what they thought best. This could be done in a series of clauses specially designed with this in mind, all of which would only come into effect if the wife died first.

The matter can be taken a stage further. The wife may literally survive her husband, but only just. What if, in that terrible accident, the husband is the one who is killed outright, while the wife is seriously injured, goes into a coma and dies a week later? As she survived her husband, she would inherit his property under his will, even though she may never have appreciated the fact. The husband's property, having passed to her under his will, would then be distributed according to her will. If she left no will, it might then pass to her relations and this could mean that all the husband's property goes to the wife's family. Also, estate duty might have to be paid twice on the same property; once on the death of the husband, and again on the death of the wife. There is a reduction in duty, known as quick succession relief, which helps a bit in this situation, but it would be far better to make provision for this possibility in advance. This could be done by providing that the wife is to receive the residue of the estate only if she survives the husband by at least 30 days. There is no magic in selecting 30 days, instead of 25 or 40, say. But if husband and wife die as a result of the same accident, it is unlikely that one would outlive the other by more than about 30 days. (If the couple own their house as joint tenants, however, a will does not affect who gets it on the death of the first to die: it passes automatically to the survivor.)

If, therefore, this formula is adopted, the main provision in the will simply says: 'I give the rest of my property to my wife, if she survives me by 30 days'. Both possibilities are then covered in the simplest way: firstly, the expected course of events of the husband dying first, leaving his wife to survive him by several years at least; and secondly, the unexpected (but possible) course of events of the wife dying first, or of their both being killed as a result of the same accident, and the wife not surviving him by at least 30 days. The will would then go on to provide for what is to happen if the wife does not survive her husband by at least 30 days.

*What to say and how to say it*

A will is chiefly concerned with disposing of property, but it can be used for some incidental matters as well. Perhaps the commonest of these, traditionally, is to specify the way in which you want your body to be disposed of: burial or cremation. You may want to leave your body to be used for medical research, your eyes for therapeutic purposes or your kidneys for transplantation. If you want this, it is more important to let your nearest relative or the person you live with know than to put it in your will.

Sometimes a guardian for young children is appointed in a will. This is more important when one parent of the children has already died. The guardian has the right to determine questions relating to the home, education and marriage of children under age.

A will is not the place for philosophical reflection, nor for expressing love, gratitude, hate, despair or any feeling about the world in general, or anyone in particular. Your will, when you are dead, will be made public, and anyone will eventually be able to see it at Somerset House, and obtain a copy of it. You may not want your private thoughts to be open to the public gaze, and it could be a source of embarrassment to your relatives if you were to explain why you left nothing to your prodigal son, or to reaffirm your love for your wife. Express your wishes simply, without embellishment, explanation or apology. If you really want to make it clear why you have left your property as you have, it is probably better to do this in an ordinary letter which can be left with the will. It is always possible that if you were to go into unnecessary detail in the will itself, you might unwittingly affect the interpretation that would be put on the words. For example, if you were to say: 'I give £500 to my cousin Robert Seaton, confident that he will do what is right by the rest of my cousins', there may be a question of whether this created a binding legal trust in favour of the other cousins. It may be that this doubt could only be resolved by an expensive court case after your death. You should instead say either: 'I give £500 to my cousin Robert Seaton' and leave it at that, or: 'I give £500 to be divided equally between . . .'.

You should aim to be precise and clear in what you say in your will. Never assume that people know what you mean; they may not, and anyway the will can only be interpreted on the basis of the words you actually use. It can happen that although a testator said one thing in his will, it is obvious that he meant something different. If this is so, the law may well stick to what he said, rather than what he meant, so strict are the rules of interpretation. For this reason also, you should avoid legal terminology, even if you feel you know the correct legal meaning. It is perfectly possible to make a will in a normal case without using technical language, so wherever it is possible, use an ordinary word and not a legal one. It

is easy to cause havoc by choosing inappropriate legal expressions. Even lawyers sometimes come unstuck by doing this, and there is a strong case for their cutting out a lot of the legal jargon they often employ in drawing wills for their clients. They use jargon partly from professional caution, resulting in a desire to use only expressions which have a tested legal meaning, or may do so partly from a desire to impress their clients. Laymen unaided should avoid legal language.

At the same time, choose your ordinary language with care. Beware of sloppy, loose expressions. If you were to say: 'I give all my money to my wife Clara', this might mean just the cash about the house, or it might mean all the cash plus what is in the bank, or it might mean everything you own. If you intend the latter, you should say: 'I give everything I own to my wife Clara'.

Often found in a home-made will is a clause which reads like this: 'I leave everything to my wife Clara; and on her death it is to be shared between my sons Albert and Sidney'. This is a disaster, and likely to have an effect quite different from what the testator intended. The point is this: if he leaves eveything to his wife Clara, so that, on his death, his property becomes her property, his will cannot then go on to say what is to happen to her property on her death. That is a matter for her to deal with in making her will. She may or may not choose to leave it to the sons Albert and Sidney. If the husband leaves his property to his wife, he cannot ordain what is to happen to it after her death (or during her lifetime, for that matter). If he does say what is to happen to it, or what remains of it on her death, the chances are that this leaves his wife with a mere life interest; that is, the right to get just the income from the property for the rest of her life, with no right to touch the capital. Of course, a husband may intend to give his wife a life interest only, in which case he should say something like this: 'I give all my property to my trustees upon trust to sell it (but with the power to postpone sale), to invest the proceeds and hold the investments on trust to pay the income to my wife Clara during her life, and on her death to divide them equally between my sons Albert and Sidney'. In such a case the widow, during the rest of her life, would have a life interest and the two sons, during her life, would have a 'reversion' giving them the property on her death. But if the husband intends that his widow should be able to do what she likes with the capital, and does not intend to restrict her to having only a life interest, he should just say: 'I give everything I own to my wife Clara', and leave her to decide what is to happen to what remains of it by the time she dies.

A later will does not automatically revoke an earlier one. There is, therefore, one more clause which should always be included in a will. This says that any previous wills are revoked. Even though you have not in fact made a will before, it is a good idea to include a statement that previous wills are revoked. Without such a clause your executors might wonder, after your death, whether perhaps you left any earlier wills. If a person leaves two wills, and they are not inconsistent with each other, they stand together. It may save your relatives a pointless search for any earlier will if you show that it is revoked anyway, and therefore no longer valid.

*Examples of wills* .

Here is an example of how a will may be prepared.

Matthew Seaton is in his thirties, is married and has two children, a boy aged six and a girl aged four. He owns his house, but he has a mortgage on it with a building society. He has an endowment policy which will produce £8,000 in 22 years' time. He owns about £300 worth of shares which are quoted on the stock exchange. He has about £500 invested with a building society, and most of the furniture and effects in the house belong to him, as well as the car. He has a bank account which is seldom in credit to the tune of more than £150. He has a steady job with an engineering company. His salary is £4,600 a year and he hopes to be earning at least £6,000 before he reaches his ceiling. His company runs a contributory pension scheme under which he will get a pension when he retires, and under which his wife Emma will receive a pension on his death, and something extra for the children if he dies while they are under 16.

Matthew is in good health and expects to live to a ripe old age. But like anyone else, he may be dead by midnight tonight, so he is making a will. The notes he makes on a scrap of paper (which he will be sure to destroy once the will is made, in case they might be confused with the will itself) might read like this:

*What I own*

(1) House: 14 Twintree Avenue, Minford

Value: say       £10,000

Subject to mortgage to Forthright Building Society; with still owing (about)    4,750

∴ net value of house to me    £5,250

(2) Endowment: worth on my death   8,000

(3) Various shares       300

(4) Amersham Building Society    300

(5) Furniture and effects in house: value as for insurance, say    900

(6) Car          650

(7) Current account at bank, say    200

          £15,600

        Call it £16,000

*Notes for will*

(1) Revoke previous wills

(2) Executors: Emma and brother David
   substitute: friend Andrew Shervington

(3) Cremation, eyes and organ transplant

(4) Bequests:

   (i) golf clubs to Donald

   (ii) cello to Daniel

   (iii) lawnmower to Rosemary Bruton

(5) Legacies:

   (i) £100 to David or Andrew, if they are my executors

   (ii) £40 to Leslie Roberts

   (iii) £100 to cancer research

(6) Residue to Emma if she survives me by 30 days
(7) If she does not, trusts for children with appropriate clauses.

Having carefully thought out how he would like to frame his will, Matthew turned his attention to the precise wording. He wrote it out in draft first. He made a few amendments to tidy up the wording, and when he was quite satisfied with it, he typed out the will itself—the engrossment, as lawyers call it—on a large piece of paper. He could have written it out by hand, but typing is better, so that there can be no question of illegibility. He decided that single spacing was the best way to type it, mainly because the whole will would then fit on to one sheet of paper, leaving sufficient room at the bottom for the signatures of himself and the witnesses. Apart from looking slightly absurd, there could be legal problems if the signatures appeared on a page by themselves. If a will extends to more than one side of a piece of paper, it is best not to break at the end of a sentence, and to leave at least one full clause for the next page. Also, the continuation should be on the back of the first piece rather than on a fresh sheet. Matthew took some pains in typing out his will, and managed to avoid making any typing errors. This is quite important, because alterations appearing on the face of a will are assumed (until the contrary is proved) to have been made after the will was signed, and so to form no part of it. If he had made any errors in preparing the engrossment, he and the witnesses would have had to authenticate the alterations by writing their initials in the margin alongside each alteration. This is what he typed:

B

WILL of Matthew John Seaton
of 14 Twintree Avenue, Minford, Surrey

1. I revoke previous wills.
2. My wife Emma and my brother David Gordon
   Seaton are to be my executors, but if either does
   not prove my will, my friend Andrew Shervington is to be an executor instead.
3. I wish my eyes and any other parts of my body
   to be used for therapeutic purposes and my
   body to be cremated.
4. I give the following bequests:
   (*a*) my golf clubs, bag and trolley to my nephew
        Donald Harrington;
   (*b*) my cello to my son Daniel;
   (*c*) my motor mower to my neighbour Mrs
        Rosemary Bruton.
5. I give the following legacies:
   (*a*) £100 to my brother David if he is an exe-
        cutor who proves my will;
   (*b*) £100 to my friend Andrew Shervington if he
        is an executor who proves my will;
   (*c*) £40 to Leslie Roberts;
   (*d*) £100 to the Imperial Cancer Research
        Fund.
6. I give to my wife Emma (if she survives me by
   30 days) the whole of the rest of my estate.
7. If she does not survive me by 30 days, the following shall apply:
   (i) I give the whole of the rest of my estate to my
       executors as trustees. They are to sell every-
       thing not in the form of cash, but they may
       postpone the sale of anything as long as they

like. After paying my debts, estate duty, and the expenses of my funeral and of administering my estate, they are to invest what is left in any type of property, just as if they were investing their own money.

(ii) My trustees are to divide my estate (including the income from it) equally between those of my children who reach the age of 18.

(iii) If any child of mine predeceases me, or dies under the age of 18, leaving children who do reach that age, then those grandchildren of mine are to divide equally between them the share of my estate which their parent would have received if that parent had lived long enough.

(iv) My trustees may buy a house and furnish it for the use of any of my children or grandchildren.

Date: . . . . . . . . . . . . . . . . . . . . . . . . . . . . . . . . .

Signature: . . . . . . . . . . . . . . . . . . . . . . . . . . .

Signed by Matthew John Seaton in our presence and by us in his: . . . . . . . . . . . . . . . . . . . . . .

. . . . . . . . . . . . . . . . . . . . . . . . . . . . . . . . . . . .

In that form Matthew Seaton's will was ready to be signed. The only part of it which was at all difficult was clause 7, the trust for the children if his wife did not survive him by at least 30 days.

There was always the possibility that he and his wife might die together before their children came of age. If this were to happen, it would not be possible for the trustees to pay out the money until each child's 18th birthday, and until then the money would have to be held on trust for them. Clause 7 (i) created what is known as a trust for sale; it is mainly intended to cover the position if there is a house, or other real property. The trustees are given a free hand to decide what should be sold and what should be kept. They are also given a free hand concerning the investment of the property for the benefit of the children. Without these words in clause 7 (i), the executors—or trustees, as they will become once they have sorted out everything following Matthew's death— would only have been able to invest the property in what are called trustee securities. These consist of stocks, shares and other investments which are so reliable that it would be unlikely that the trustees would lose the money. Only gilt-edged securities (those where payment is guaranteed by the government), the larger building societies and public companies, and similar safe investments are included. You may, of course, prefer that these restrictions on the trustees' power to invest your property should apply in your case. If so, you will leave out all the words in clause 7 (i), after '. . . invest what is left'. But people often prefer to widen these legal powers of investment. Some wills contain a clause setting out the sort of investments that may be used. If you have complete confidence in your trustees, you can do as Matthew has done: remove all restrictions on their power to invest your property. You leave it to their judgment, trusting that they will take good advice from experts, to choose whatever is best. With this unlimited power to invest your property, they could, if they liked, put some of your money into some highly speculative venture, and lose it.

Clause 7 (ii) provides that the children are to share the estate equally. But this would depend on each one becoming 18. It is not essential to add this requirement, but it is commonly done. One reason is to guard against the fecklessness of youth. If one of your children, at 16, knew that he was entitled, come what may, to a share in an estate, he might blue the lot in advance on riotous living. You guard against this to some extent by providing that he is not eligible for a share until he becomes 18. This makes it more difficult for him even to raise a loan on the strength of his inheritance, for if he were to die between 16 and 18, say, his share would be worth nothing. But though he may never in fact reach 18 and inherit, he can get a share in the income of the property, before he comes of age. The trustees can, if they like, use the income that is received from the investments to help meet the cost of maintaining and educating the children. Any income they do not use for this would be accumulated, invested, and ultimately distributed, with the capital of the estate, as each child becomes 18. In 1970 the age of 18 was substituted for 21 as the age at which a young person comes of age. But a parent can still stipulate 21 years, or any other age, as the age at which his children shall receive his property.

Some of the capital of the estate, also, can be used to help with the maintenance or education of the children, even while they are still minors. Up to half of each one's expected share in the capital can be used in this way. Take an example: imagine that Matthew Seaton is killed, with his wife Emma, in an accident, and that he leaves the residue of his estate worth £16,000 on trust for any of his children who reach the age of 18. When he made his will he had two children. At the time of his death he has four, aged 11, 9, 5 and 3. The £16,000 would be invested for them, and the income from it (£800 a year, if invested at 5 per cent) could be used for their maintenance and education. Each one would expect to receive £4,000 when he or she reached 18. If any one of them died before that, his or her share would be divided between the surviving three equally. But in spite of the risk of this happening, it is still open to the trustees, if they want to, to use up to £2,000 of the capital for helping with the maintenance or education of each one of them: half of each one's expected share. And if one of the children for whom that was done then died before his 18th birthday, and so never really got to the stage of inheriting his share, nevertheless no part of the advance made to him would have to be paid back to the others.

The hypothesis in clause 7 (iii) is that one at least of the children might die under the age of 18 (without having become absolutely entitled to his share), and yet have already married and had a child of his own: a grandchild of Matthew Seaton, in the example. In that case, if there were no clause 7 (iii), the grandchild would get nothing. Clause 7 (iii) provides that the grandchild inherits the share which, but for earlier death, his father (or mother) would have inherited on his (or her) 18th birthday. In relation to a child over 18 who died before his father, leaving children, it is likewise necessary to say that these grandchildren are to get their parent's share, and clause 7 (iii) does this. All this may seem very far removed from reality, when Matthew is sitting down now, about to sign his

will, with two healthy children noisily around him.
His own death is sufficiently unthinkable. The death
of one of his children leaving a baby grandchild
behind is hardly to be contemplated. But it is sensible
to provide for what may conceivably happen in the
future.

Lastly, clause 7 (iv) gives the trustees a special
power to buy a house, and if necessary to furnish it,
for the benefit of Matthew's children and grandchildren. This could be useful to the trustees in some
cases. To buy a house is not clearly within their
investment powers as set out in clause 7 (i): 'to invest
what is left in any type of property . . .', because to
buy a house for the children to live in is not, strictly
speaking, investing the money, there being no income
coming in as a result. To be able to buy a house out
of the estate, and to furnish it, needs a special power
and this clause confers it. There may be no immediate
problem while the home—the one where the family is
living at the time of the death—is retained for the
children to use. The problem would arise if that one
were sold, and the trustees wanted to buy another,
perhaps smaller one, for the children to live in. This
they could only do with such a clause.

The will was now ready for signature. Before considering the way to sign it, take two more examples of
how to draw a will.

Many people do not have young children to consider, and the comparatively complicated clause 7 in
Matthew Seaton's will would, therefore, not need to
appear at all. Quite often a person wishes to leave all
his property to one other person, with no complications. A man whose children are grown up may wish

to leave all his property to his wife. He may not wish to provide for the possibility of his wife and himself being killed together (the children would share the estate, anyway) or giving his wife a mere life interest in his estate, with a view to saving some estate duty on the wife's subsequent death. In his case, the simplest possible will would do. It would also be suitable for an unmarried man or woman who wished to leave everything to one other adult, a brother or friend, perhaps. In that situation, the will merely needs to leave everything to the one person, and that person should be appointed to be the executor. It could read like this:

> Will of Margaret Ellen Seaton, of 12 Chiltern Court, Foden Gardens, Hastings, Sussex.
>
> I revoke previous wills. I appoint my brother Matthew John Seaton of 14 Twintree Avenue, Minford, Surrey, to be the sole executor of this will, and leave to him everything I own.
>
> Date: . . . . . . . . . . . . . . . . . . . . . . . . . . . . . . . .
>
> Signature:  . . . . . . . . . . . . . . . . . . . . . . . . . . . . .
>
> Signed by Margaret Ellen Seaton in our presence, and by us in hers:  . . . . . . . . . . . . . . . . . . . . . . .
>
> . . . . . . . . . . . . . . . . . . . . . . . . . . . . . . . . . . .

A wife should make a will, just as much as a husband should. The amount a person has to leave is not particularly relevant to the question of whether he or she should make a will. Each should make a will.

Husband and wife sometimes make their wills together and at the same time. When this happens, they often make their wills complementary, the one being the mirror image of the other.

*. . . the one being the mirror-image of the other*

Let us suppose that Matthew Seaton's wife Emma made her will at the same time as he made his. It would read something like this:

Will of Emma Seaton of 14 Twintree Avenue, Minford, Surrey.

1. I revoke previous wills.
2. I appoint my husband Matthew John Seaton and my cousin Edward Seymour Forbes to be the executors of my will. If either does not prove my will, I appoint my brother-in-law David Gordon Seaton to be an executor instead.
3. I wish my body to be buried.
4. If my husband Matthew survives me by 30 days, I give him all my property.
5. If he does not survive me by 30 days, the following shall apply:
    (i) I give the whole of my estate to my executors as trustees. They are to sell everything not in the form of cash, but they may postpone the sale of anything as long as they like. After paying my debts, estate duty, and the expenses of my funeral and of

administering my estate, they are to invest what is left in any type of property, just as if they were investing their own money.

(ii) My trustees are to divide my estate, including the income from it, equally between those of my children who reach the age of 18.

(iii) If any child of mine predeceases me, or dies under the age of 18, leaving children who do reach that age, then those grandchildren of mine are to divide equally between them the share of my estate which their parent would have received, if that parent had lived long enough.

(iv) My trustees may buy a house and furnish it for the use of any of my children or grandchildren.

Date: . . . . . . . . . . . . . . . . . . . . . . . . . . . .

Signature: . . . . . . . . . . . . . . . . . . . . . . .

Signed by Emma Seaton in our presence, and by us in hers: . . . . . . . . . . . . . . . . . .

. . . . . . . . . . . . . . . . . . . . . . . . . . . . . . . .

She appoints someone on her side of the family—her cousin—to be an executor with her husband. She does not have to, and if there is any fear of antagonism between them, it is probably better to have someone who gets on with the husband. The substitute executor is in this case the husband's brother. She could easily have appointed Matthew to be sole executor, with a provision that her cousin and brother-in-law should be her executors if Matthew did not prove her will.

*Signing the will*

A will does not have to state the date on which it was signed, but it is much better that it should. The date can appear at the beginning or the end, it does not matter which. Perhaps if it is at the end, just above the place for signing, there is slightly less chance of forgetting to fill in the date when the will is actually signed. Lawyers tend to set out the date in full 'the twenty-seventh day of June one thousand nine hundred and seventy-two'. Even 'in the year of Our Lord . . .' is not completely extinct today. There is nothing wrong with putting '27 June 1972', provided it is written legibly in the space on the will meant for it. The date may be put in without any witnesses being present.

Anyone who is left anything in the will should not be a witness, and neither should the wife or husband of anyone who is left anything in it. Where this happens, the will is legally valid—in other words, these witnesses are perfectly all right as witnesses—but they lose their legacies; the will is interpreted as if the gift to the witness, or the spouse of the witness, were cut out of it. Secondly, a blind person should not be a witness. Also, it is probably best to avoid having someone under age to be a witness, although there is nothing in law about it.

The will must be signed by the testator, the person whose will it is, within the sight of two witnesses, who must both be present together.

It will be invalid unless both the witnesses are physically present when the will is signed, although, strictly speaking it is still a valid will if the testator acknowledges his previously written signature—as distinct from signing there and then—in the joint presence of the two witnesses. It is best that they should both actually watch as the signature goes on, although it is sufficient if they are standing or sitting in such a position that they could have seen the signing, if they had looked in the right direction. The testator must sign first, and the witnesses afterwards; the other way round will not do. Each witness must sign in the presence of the testator. If Matthew Seaton were to sign his will in the presence of Robert Jones and Michael Smith, and then, before either of them began to sign, Matthew went out of the room, and while he was out of the room, Robert and Michael signed as witnesses, the will would be invalid. The same would apply if only one of the witnesses signed out of the presence of the testator. But it does not matter if one of the witnesses is out of the room when the other witness is signing.

To sum up, then: the person making the will must be there all the time that anybody is signing; both the witnesses must be there when the testator signs; it is not necessary for each witness to be present when the other witness signs. To be on the safe side, however, the best thing is to make sure that all three of them are present throughout all the signing by all three of them.

The will should contain an attestation clause, that is, a clause explaining the process of signing and witnessing. If the clause were missing, then, after the testator's death, when it comes to proving the will, it would be necessary to have an affidavit—a sworn statement—from one of the witnesses to explain what happened when the will was signed and witnessed.

This could cause great difficulties if the witnesses cannot be traced, or are dead. So a properly worded attestation clause, though not strictly necessary, should be included in a will.

Lawyers tend to favour rather a long attestation clause. One often finds something like this: 'Signed by the said Matthew John Seaton as and for his last will and testament in the presence of us both present at the same time, who at his request, in his presence and in the presence of each other have hereunto sub-scribed our names as witnesses.' But it is enough just to say: 'Signed by Matthew John Seaton in our pre-sence, and by us in his'.

It is also not strictly necessary for the witnesses to write their addresses on the will. Their signatures are all that is legally required. But, once again, it is much better if they do add their address, and perhaps their occupation as well, so that if there were any questions raised later about what happened at the time, they can more easily be traced. For the same reason, if either of their signatures is such as to make their surname illegible, it is not a bad idea to write the name in block letters underneath the signature.

If your will runs to more than one page, it is a good idea to sign each page at the bottom, and to ask the two witnesses to do the same. This is not a legal requirement, but it does help to prevent any forgery of your will, in the form of adding a clause to the bottom of a page, for instance. If, after your death, a clause saying 'I give £5,000 to William Sykes' appeared at the foot of a page, you would not be there to explain that it was not there when you signed the will. Signing each page is more important still when the will extends to more than one sheet of paper. It is better not to leave blank the back page of any sheet of paper on which your will is written. Either continue with the clauses on to the back of each page, or draw a line right across the blank space, and put your initials at the top and bottom of the line. Ask the witnesses to do the same. It should be your aim to make any tampering with your will as difficult as possible, and at the same time make it obvious which are the sheet of paper which comprise your will, each sheet of which should bear your signature at the bottom. Make sure that each page of your will is numbered, so that no one can craftily slip in a couple of extra pages containing benefits to himself. Finally, do not pin anything to your will and make sure that no pin holes appear in it. Such holes may give the impression that a sheet of paper forming part of your will was at one time attached to it, but has now disappeared.

When the process of signing and witnessing is over, how then does the will appear? Take the examples already considered. Picking up Matthew Seaton's will at the last part of the last clause as it was prepared, it will now continue through to the end to look like this:

(iv) My trustees may buy a house and furnish it for the use of any of my children or grand-children.

Date: 27 June 1972.
Signature: M. J. Seaton.

Signed by Matthew John Seaton in our presence
and by us in his:

| Robert A. Jones | M. B. Smith |
|---|---|
| 22 Twintree Avenue | 'The Reddings', Park Avenue, |
| Minford, Surrey. | Minford, Surrey |
| Sales Manager. | Schoolmaster. |

His sister's will when signed and witnessed would
look like this:

Will of Margaret Ellen Seaton, of 12 Chiltern
Court, Foden Gardens, Hastings, Sussex.
I revoke previous wills. I appoint my brother Matthew John Seaton of 14 Twintree Avenue, Minford, Surrey, to be the sole executor of this will,
and leave to him everything I own.
Date: 6 July 1972.
Signature: Margaret E. Seaton.
Signed by Margaret Ellen Seaton in our presence,
and by us in hers:

| Ivy Gurney | Daniel Wedmore |
|---|---|
| 'The Larches', London Grove | 88 Abraham Street |
| Eastbourne. | Hastings. |
| Bookseller. | Milkman. |

From the moment the will is signed and witnessed
it is valid. Matthew and Margaret Seaton may safely
die at any time, secure in the knowledge that their
testamentary wishes have been legally expressed.

There is no law in England and Wales requiring
that wills must be registered before death, at the
moment. As a result, it is up to the testator himself to
find a safe place for his will, to put it there, and to let

his relatives know where it is. Quite a few people lodge their will in their bank. If you have a safe at home, this is an obvious place in which to put your will. Failing that, perhaps the best place for your will is wherever you keep your other important documents: marriage and birth certificates, savings certificates, title deeds of the house, and so on. Put the will in an envelope, sealing it if you want to, and write on the outside your full name, the word WILL in large letters and the date. There is no stamp duty on a will, so no further formalities are required to be met before putting the will away safely.

Besides telling your immediate relatives where your will is, you should tell your executors where it is, too. Tell them when the will has been made, and confirm that the will appoints them as executors. If the will is locked away, tell them where the key is. Whether or not you tell your executors, and indeed your relatives, who is going to inherit your property under your will is entirely up to you; there is no legal requirement. But you should keep your executors informed about what you possess. A list, setting out in round figures what you own, could well be placed with your will for safe custody, and from time to time you should revise the list to keep it up to date. You should, perhaps, have told your executors, when asking whether they were willing to accept the appointment, what your property consisted of and its approximate value, so that they knew in advance what was the measure of the job they were being asked to take on. As time goes by, and your situation develops and changes, they should be kept informed of how your current wealth stands, especially if you acquire unusual assets. Your object should be to make things as easy as possible for them when you die. Any tendency to be secretive about your assets is only likely to make life more difficult for your executors.

You should also keep them up to date on where the essential documents are to be found. The logical course, obviously, is to keep things like share certificates, building society share accounts, savings books, savings certificates, insurance policies, title deeds and all similar documents in one place, a family safe, for instance, or a locked drawer, maybe. This is probably the same place as where your will itself is kept. If you keep your affairs tidy and orderly so far as possible, when the time comes for your executors to act, they will not find that they have taken on an investigation, instead of an administration. It may be tomorrow.

*You should have told your executors what your property consisted of.*

*Alterations*

Any obvious alterations made on the face of a will are presumed—until the contrary is proved—to have been made after the original signing and witnessing took place, and so not to form part of the legally valid will. Furthermore, any legacy which appears underneath your signature is not valid.

You may want to alter your will, owing to a change in circumstances, such as a death, or a change of heart following a difference of opinion, for instance. You must not cross bits out of your will, or write bits in, or make any alterations whatsoever on it. The will is valid in the form in which it stood on the day it was signed. Theoretically, you could make subsequent alterations on the will itself by signing the altered will and having that new signature witnessed again, as was done when the will was first signed. But this is messy and unsatisfactory, and quite the wrong way to go about making alterations to a will.

If all you want to do is to make a simple alteration to your will as it stands, you could do this by making a codicil. This really is nothing more than a supplement to a will, which makes some alteration to it but leaves the rest of it standing. For instance, you may wish to increase the cash legacy, to take account of inflation since you made the will. To find out the whole of the testator's wishes, both the will and the codicil have to be considered. A codicil, to be valid, must be signed and witnessed in exactly the same way as a will. It has to be signed by the testator in the presence of two witnesses and they must both sign it in the presence of the testator. These witnesses do not have to be the same two who witnessed the original will. Here is an example:

This is the first codicil to the will, dated 27 June 1972, of me Matthew John Seaton of 14 Twintree Avenue, Minford, Surrey.

1. I revoke the bequest of my golf clubs, bag and trolley to my nephew Donald Harrington.
2. I give £250 to my brother Robert Seaton.
3. In all other respects I confirm my will.

Date: 5 October 1972.
Signature: M. J. Seaton.

Signed by Matthew John Seaton in our presence and by us in his:

| | |
|---|---|
| Ivy Gurney | Brian Warshaw |
| 'The Larches', | 140 Latchmoor Grove |
| London Grove, | Gerrards Cross, Bucks. |
| Eastbourne. | Company Director. |
| Bookseller. | |

Some people make quite a few codicils. There is no limit on how many you may make. But a codicil is only suitable for a straightforward alteration to a will. For anything more than that it is better to make a completely new will. If the will was quite short in the first place, it is probably better to make a completely new will anyway, and not bother with making a codicil.

*Revocation*

If you make a later will, it should, of course, contain the clause which revokes the previous will. Once the

later will is signed, and so in force, it is best to des
troy the previous one, just in case, years later whe
you die, the old will is found among your papers, an
mistaken for the one you meant to apply.

There are two other ways of revoking a wi
besides a specific clause in a later will mentionin
revocation. The first is where, with the intention
revoking it, you burn it, tear it up, or in some othe
way destroy it. The emphasis here is on the word
'with the intention of revoking it'. If your will were t
be accidentally burnt, whether by you or by someon
else, it would not be revoked by that. There have, i
fact, been cases where a will has been declared vali
after the testator's death, the original having bee
accidentally destroyed. In one case, for instance, th
torn up pieces were reassembled and proved as
valid will, where it was shown that it was torn up
mistake for an old letter. The testator himself mu
burn the will, or tear it up, in order for it to be effe
tively revoked. Alternatively, it may be done t
someone at his direction and in his presence. Yo
will would not be revoked, for example, if you we
to write to the bank manager who kept it, telling hi
to destroy it, even if he did so. The destruction has
take place in your presence and if this does not ha
pen the will is not revoked until, of course, a subs
quent will is made which contains a revocati
clause.

＼ The other way of revoking a will is the most su
prising and the one that is most easily forgotten: ge
ting married. The law supposes that a man or
woman who has made a will and later gets marri
automatically wishes that the will should no long

stand. As a result, merely to get married, without saying anything about an existing will, revokes the will. This can have some curious results. Imagine that a widow with young children has made a will leaving her property to the children. Some years later she marries again. She must make a new will after the second marriage, otherwise her new husband will inherit up to £15,000 of her property, as she would have died intestate, her will having been revoked by her second marriage. Divorce, on the other hand, does not automatically revoke a will. You should, therefore, make a new will if your marriage has been dissolved.

It is however possible to make a will which says that it is made in contemplation of a forthcoming marriage. Such a will is not revoked by that marriage.

Once you have made a will, it is easy to tuck it away safely and forget about it for ever. But you should review your will now and again; roughly every five years is about the right interval. You may find that nothing needs changing. On the other hand, there could be quite substantial changes that need to be made. If so, you will have to start the whole process over again.

In Scotland

*In Scotland any minor child (that is a girl over 12 or a boy over 14) can make a will.*

*A will which has been signed before two witnesses is, as in England, valid. But if the will is written on two or more sheets of paper it must be signed at the foot of each page by the testator. The witnesses however, need sign only the last page. It is not essential for the witnesses to see the testator signing—it would be enough if the testator acknowledged to the witnesses that this was in fact his signature. But a long delay in acknowledging the signature might invalidate the will and it is by far the best thing to make sure that the testator and both witnesses all sign at the same time.*

*The will must show the full names, occupation and addresses of the witnesses and it is usual to add to the end of the will a clause giving these details. It is the equivalent of an english attestation clause, but is called, in Scotland, a testing clause. Often the date and place of signing are added here, though this is not absolutely necessary. The testing clause would then look like this:*

*'In witness whereof I have subscribed this will written on this and the two preceding pages at Edinburgh on the twenty-eighth day of June nineteen hundred and seventy-two before these witnesses, Robert Arthur Jones, sales manager, twenty-two Crawley Avenue, Edinburgh, and Martin Bertram Smith, schoolmaster, eleven Boevey Street, Edinburgh.'*

*If a testing clause is not added then the witnesses should write their occupations and addresses after their signatures.*

*Any alterations or additions made to the will should be noted in the testing clause:*

'In witness whereof I have subscribed this will consisting of this and the preceding page and the marginal addition on page two which is to be read after the word. . . .' *The marginal addition also has to be initialled by the testator.*

None of this differs very much from England. Unlike english law, however, scots law accepts as valid a will which is holograph of the testator: entirely in his handwriting and signed by him. If the will is holograph, no witnesses are necessary. But it is no good writing only part of the will in your own handwriting if the rest of it is typed or printed. This would not necessarily be holograph. For example, if you buy a will form from a stationer, you will probably find that bits of the will have already been printed out for you and you are expected to fill in the blanks. If you do this and sign the form, it is not necessarily holograph—to make it a valid will you would have to have it witnessed in the usual way. Alternatively, you could adopt the printing as if it were your own writing. If you write the words 'adopted as holograph' in your own handwriting on the form and sign it, the will would be treated as if the whole thing had in fact been written out entirely in your hand. If you have any doubt whether your will is holograph, the safest course is to have it witnessed.

A will which has been witnessed proves itself. A holograph will, on the other hand, has to be proved to be in the handwriting of the testator before confirmation can be granted. This is done by producing affidavits from two people who were acquainted with the handwriting of the testator.

*An english will is revoked by the subsequent marriage of the testator. A scottish will is not. On the other hand if a scotsman makes a will which does not mention children as yet unborn and subsequently a child is born to the testator, then that will is presumed to be revoked.*

*It is difficult for a scotsman to disinherit his wife and children because they have on his death certain rights (usually termed 'legal rights'). These rights which have to be satisfied out of the moveable estate of the deceased are as follows:*

jus relictae, *which is the right of a widow to one half of her husband's moveable estate if there are no children and one third if there are* (jus relecti *is the equivalent right of a widower to one half or one third of his wife's moveable estate*);

legitim, *which is the right of the children to one half of the moveable estate of their father (or of their mother) if the other parent is already dead, or one third if the other parent survives.*

*These rights can be claimed if a scotsman or scotswoman dies intestate. But even if he or she leaves a valid will, legal rights can still be claimed in spite of that will. Accordingly, it is not possible wholly to disinherit a surviving spouse or surviving children—all that can safely be left to others if the surviving spouse or children choose to contest the will, is the 'dead's part', that is what is left after deducting legal rights. On the other hand, it is not possible for a child or spouse to claim legal rights and at the same time to accept the provisions made for him or her in a will. The child or spouse mus* choose between his or her legal rights and his or her rights under the will.

Legal rights may sometimes be got around. They can only be claimed out of moveable estate. If the deceased leaves mainly heritable property (*that is land and house*), there may be very little out of which to claim legal rights. Also, if you die intestate, the law allows the surviving spouse certain 'prior rights' which may be so extensive as to swallow up all the moveable estate and leave nothing out of which the children may claim legitim or any other of their rights on intestacy. So, paradoxically, if you do want to disinherit your children you may best be able to do that by dying intestate.

The people who deal with what you own when you die are called your personal representatives. If they are appointed by a valid will, they are known as executors; when they were not appointed in this way, as happens on an intestacy, the personal representatives are known as administrators.

In either case, they usually have to obtain an official document from the High Court to show that they are the ones with legal authority to deal with the property. In the case of executors, who are said to prove the will, this document is called a grant of probate, also referred to as probate of the will, or, for short, the probate. Administrators, on the other hand, obtain a grant of letters of administration. The document which constitutes the probate or the letters of administration is sometimes referred to as the grant. The task of executors as well as of administrators is referred to as the administration of the estate.

It is not always essential to take out a grant of probate or letters of administration. If the property left behind consists only of cash (that is bank notes and coins) and personal effects such as furniture and a car (and not, for instance, any shares, bank accounts, pension arrears or house), no formal steps to prove the right of the relatives to their inheritance need be taken. They can immediately take physical possession of everything. But the will should never be destroyed. Of course, if there is a dispute amongst them as to who shall have what, or how it is to be organised, it may be necessary to put the whole matter on a proper legal footing by taking out a grant.

There are some other kinds of property which can be handed over without much formality. Where, for instance, the deceased held not more than £500 in national savings with the Department for National Savings, that amount (together with the interest to the date of payment) can be paid to the person now entitled to it, without a grant being taken out at all. The same applies to money held in other savings banks, friendly societies and certain pension funds. The sum involved in the savings bank (or similar) must not exceed £500, but the total value of the estate (including the money in the savings bank) may be more than £500. The procedure for obtaining the money is usually simple. The relative entitled to claim the money writes to the savings bank or other organisation concerned, explaining the circumstances, and asking to be sent the appropriate form. This must then be completed and returned with the 15p death certificate ('certificate for certain statutory purposes') and, where appropriate, the marriage certificate. (However, the savings bank or other body can, at its discretion, require you to take out a grant even if the amount involved is under £500.)

There is a system of nominating some kinds of property in favour of a particular person, to take effect on death. In the case of a National Savings Bank account, for instance, a person who wishes to nominate the money in it has to obtain the nomination form (from the National Savings Bank, Glasgow G58 1SB), fill it in, sign it (in the presence of a witness who must also sign the form) and return it there for registration. National savings certificates are nominated on a different form, which is obtained from, and registered with, The Director of Savings, Savings Certificate and SAYE Office, Millburngate

House, Durham DH99 1NS. British Savings Bonds and government stock on the National Savings Stock Register can be nominated on a form obtainable from the Director of Savings, Bonds and Stock Office, Lytham St Annes, Lancs FY0 1YN. Premium savings bonds and save-as-you-earn contracts cannot be nominated.

The person to whom savings are nominated in this way can apply to have them in cash or transferred into his name on producing the death certificate, and without producing a grant of probate or letters of administration. This procedure for nomination is quite distinct from the procedure for obtaining payment in cases under £500, and applies irrespective of the amount involved, provided that there has been a nomination. If the value of the property nominated exceeds £3,000, the savings bank may require a certificate from the Inland Revenue to show that estate duty has been taken care of. A nomination made in this way applies whether or not a will mentions it and is not revoked or affected by a will made afterwards. A nomination is revoked by signing the special form, or by a marriage, or by the death of the person in whose favour the nomination was made before the death of the person who made it.

Nomination cannot be made for the contents of a Giro account.

*What is involved*

In most cases, an administration by personal representatives follows roughly this pattern:

Find out the nature and value of the estate.

Find out details of the debts.

Prepare a detailed list of the estate and of the debts, for the purpose of estate duty.

Work out roughly the amount of estate duty and arrange any necessary overdraft or other credit.

Prepare the documents required by the probate registry.

Swear the documents.

Pay the estate duty.

Receive the grant of probate or letters of administration.

Send the grant, or a photocopy of it, to the bank, the insurance company, and so on.

Collect together the estate.

Sell any property.

Pay the debts.

Pay the legacies.

Hand over the bequests.

Distribute or invest the residue.

Any one of a number of complexities can arise in connection with winding up an estate. Many personal representatives would not contemplate administering an estate without employing a solicitor. They are often busy people, without the time to cope with the legal side of an administration. In many cases, a solicitor's services are essential: when the deceased owned his own business, for instance, or was a partner in a firm, or when family trusts are involved (stemming from the deceased's parents, perhaps, or from a marriage settlement). If the deceased left no will and the estate comes to more than £15,000, after deducting the value of the personal effects including the car, the spouse will get a life interest, provided that there are children as well. In this case the complications likely to arise from the life interest make a solicitor's advice and help almost essential. The same applies where, on an intestacy or under the will, some of the property is to pass to children who are at present under age. Their rights are called minority interests, and particular legal problems can arise regarding them. This is so whether the children are 17 weeks, 17 months or 17 years old.

Another situation which usually demands consulting a solicitor is where, on an intestacy, some long forgotten relative is entitled to a share in the estate. For example, a brother—perhaps the black sheep of the family—may have gone to Australia 40 years ago and not been heard of since. In such a case. the australian brother is entitled, if the deceased left no will, to the same share as the sister who lovingly nursed the deceased through his last years of illness. The problems involved in tracing relatives who have apparently disappeared generally require expert handling, as does the situation if they are not in fact found.

Home-made wills, particularly those made on some of the printed will forms, sometimes contain ambiguities or irregularities which can create difficulties.

*. . . some long-forgotten relative entitled to a share . . .*

Even if a court case about the interpretation of the will can be avoided, legal help may be needed at some stage.

If the estate is insolvent—if the debts exceed the value of the assets—a solicitor needs to be consulted. The same applies where, although the estate is solvent, there is not sufficient to pay all the legacies in full; that is, where there is no residue.

A solicitor's fees for dealing with an estate are paid out of the deceased's property. They are a proper expense, like the funeral expenses, and the estate duty; the personal representatives do not have to pay them out of their own pockets. But they have to be paid nevertheless, and it is normally the residuary legatee who bears them. He is the person who, under the will, is to receive the rest of the deceased's property after paying out everything else, including these expenses and the legacies of fixed amounts.

The amount charged by solicitors for work of this kind depends on a number of factors, including the amount of work involved, the urgency of the case and the value of the estate. There are not many estates where the solicitor's fees will be less than £100, and in a large number of cases they will be much more. There is no recommended scale fee where the gross estate is under £2,000. Where the gross estate is worth £2,000 or more, the Law Society recommends the following scale as an appropriate basis for fees in normal probate cases: on a gross estate between £2,000 and £10,000, a rate of 3 per cent of the gross estate; on the next £40,000 (that is, between £10,000 and £50,000), $2\frac{1}{2}$ per cent of the gross estate; lower rates apply above that. So on a £12,000 estate, the personal representatives might expect to have to pay solicitors' fees of about £350. In addition, there are probate registry fees, commissioners' fees for oaths, and other out of pocket expenses to be paid, not to mention the estate duty. These expenses have to be paid, whether a solicitor is instructed or not. But the fees paid to the solicitor can be saved if the personal representatives deal with the administration of the estate themselves.

There are precedents for people going about some enterprise which is generally the province of the legal profession, but without in fact having any assistance from that direction. Some have taken court cases alone, litigants in person, as they are called. Many laymen have bought a house without a solicitor, although some have found that there is more to it than they expected. Whereas the litigant in person and the do-it-yourself house buyer must feel their way uncertainly through the devious ways the lawyers have made for themselves, the personal representative will find that there is a special machinery set up just for him. There is a personal application department in each of the probate registries, which has special staff special forms and special procedures designed to smooth the path of the inexperienced layman. He is in fact, unlikely to run across solicitors in the course of his administration, and the officials he encounter are likely to be friendly and helpful. But the help and advice given by the personal application department of a probate registry is confined to getting the grant of probate or letters of administration, and the personal representative is generally left to find out for himself—by reading this book, for instance—what goes before and what comes after.

## The administration of an estate

Herbert Blake has died. Mary Blake his widow, and Matthew Seaton his son-in-law, are his executors. Matthew and his mother-in-law have agreed that they will not instruct a solicitor in connection with the administration of the estate of her late husband. This is the story of what they did.

Matthew is the businesslike member of the family, and it was natural that he took charge of events. Matthew had known of his appointment as one of the executors, but had never been shown the will itself. The will had been drawn up by a solicitor and put in the Blakes' deed box.

Matthew read the will at once to see what it said about burial or cremation. He had no intention of arranging a formal reading of the will to the family after the funeral. This ritual happens mostly in the world of fiction.

## Herbert Blakes's will

THIS IS THE LAST WILL AND TESTAMENT of me HERBERT GEORGE BLAKE of The Firs, Willow Lane, Minford, Surrey, Factory Manager.

I hereby revoke all former wills and codicils at any time heretofore made by me and declare this to be my last will and testament.

1. I hereby appoint my Dear Wife MARY JOSEPHINE BLAKE and my son-in-law MATTHEW JOHN SEATON of 38 Broadstone Drive, Hastings, in the County of Sussex, to be the executors and trustees of this my will.

2. I bequeath the grandfather clock which I inherited from my father to my son Robert Anthony Blake.
3. I give to my daughter Mrs. Emma Seaton the sum of £500, and to each of my two sons, that is to the said Robert Anthony Blake and to Mark Douglas Blake, the sum of £750.
4. Subject to the payment of my just debts, funeral and testamentary expenses and any duties payable on my death, I give devise and bequeath all the rest residue and remainder of my estate both real and personal whatsoever and wheresoever situate unto my trustees UPON TRUST to sell the same (but with power in their absolute discretion to postpone such sale) and to hold the net proceeds of the sale together with the net rents and profits to arise therefrom until sale UPON TRUST for my Wife the said MARY JOSEPHINE BLAKE for her own use and benefit absolutely.
5. I express the wish that my body may be cremated and that my ashes shall be scattered.

IN WITNESS whereof I have hereunto set my hand this sixteenth day of August One thousand nine hundred and fifty-seven.

Herbert G. Blake.

Signed by the above named Testator HERBERT GEORGE BLAKE as for his last Will and Testament in the presence of us both present together who at his request in his presence and in the presence of each other have hereunto subscribed our names as witnesses:

| Roland M. Dodds | David B. Mackenzie |
| 1 Charter Street | his Clerk. |
| Minford, Surrey. | |
| Solicitor. | |

This was a will prepared by a solicitor. In 1957, when it was signed, all three of the testator's children were under age, so it might have included a clause to deal with the possibility of husband and wife being killed together, or at any rate of his wife dying first. Matthew suspected that the reason why no such clause appeared was that Herbert Blake had rejected the idea, rather than that the solicitor had not suggested it. Mary Blake was eight years younger than her husband, and he had thought that he would die first. He had been right.

Matthew was struck by the uneconomical use of language. The will in effect said that Mrs Blake was to have everything, except for the legacies to the three children.

In the deed box Matthew found a number of other documents, including a life insurance policy, some national savings certificates, a National Savings Bank book, and a few share certificates. Matthew put them back into the box, together with the will, and took the box home.

From the contents of the will, Matthew had satisfied himself that he had full authority to act as an executor with his mother-in-law. A valid will operates from the moment of its maker's death, so that an executor has full authority from the moment of a person's death. That authority is effective, even though the will has not yet been formally proved in the way the law demands. When eventually the will is proved, by the issue to the executors of a grant of probate, it merely confirms and makes official the powers they have had since death. This is an important distinction between probate and letters of administration; administrators have no legal authority to act until the grant of letters of administration is issued to them.

It was obvious to Matthew that his mother-in-law, his co-executor, would want him to deal with the business side of the executorship, and to leave all the formalities to him. But he made a point of specifically asking her to confirm that this was so. Apart from the courtesy of doing so, this was legally the correct thing to do. She was as much an executor as he was, and the proper procedure was for both of them to authorise him to make the necessary arrangements on behalf of both of them.

The next formality Matthew attended to was the registration of the death of Herbert Blake with the registrar of births and deaths. Having registered the death, Matthew obtained copies of the various death certificates he would be needing on several occasions in the next few weeks.

Within a few days Matthew had assembled most of the available documents regarding the late Herbert Blake's property. He started to prepare a list of all the items, with an estimate of the value of each. He was able, from the documents he had found in the house, together with information from his mother-in-law, to compile a provisional list of the assets which made up the estate, estimating high rather than low where he was doubtful.

| *Herbert George Blake* | | £ |
|---|---|---|
| *Provisional details of the estate* | | |
| National Savings Bank Account (plus interest to date of death) | | 400 |
| Savings certificates | | 1,000 |
| Various stocks and shares (to be valued, but say approximately) | | 12,000 |
| House: The Firs, Willow Lane, Minford (say) | £18,000 | |
| Less outstanding on mortgage (about) | 800 | |
| | | 17,200 |
| Contents of house, inc. furniture | | 1,000 |
| Car | | 1,350 |
| Bank account: Barminster Bank, Minford (about) | | 200 |
| Insurance policy (plus profits) | | 3,500 |
| Balance of pension | | 10 |
| Other odds and ends (say) | | 200 |
| | *approximate gross estate* | 36,860 |
| *Debts* | | |
| Funeral | 120 | |
| Miscellaneous | 100 | |
| | | 220 |
| | *approximate net estate* | 36,640 |
| Estate duty (approx.) | | 1,700 |
| | | 34,940 |
| Probate fees and other expenses, allow | | 80 |
| Approximate value to divide according to the will: | | 34,860 |

*Valuation of assets*

Matthew now had a good idea of what was likely to be involved in administering the estate. He prepared a letter to write to the Department for National Savings, the bank manager, and the insurance company, to find out the precise value of some of the assets:

Dear Sir,

*Herbert George Blake deceased*

I am an executor of the will of the late Herbert George Blake, who died on 12 May 1972; my co-executor is his widow, Mrs Mary Josephine Blake of 'The Firs', Willow Lane, Minford, which is the late Mr Blake's address.

The estate includes the asset described below. Please let me know the value of this asset at the date of death.

When the grant of probate has been obtained, I shall send it, or an official copy of it, to you for your inspection. Please let me know what formalities (if any) will be involved in obtaining payment of what is due to the estate.

*Particulars of asset:*

Name in which held:

Description of asset:

Reference number:

Estimated amount or value: £

Additional information required:

Yours faithfully,

In the letter he sent to the Director, National Savings Bank, Glasgow G58 1SB, he completed the particulars to read as follows:

*Particulars of asset:*
Name in which held: Herbert George Blake
Description of asset: National Savings Bank
account
Reference number: George Street, Croydon,
No. 5441
Estimated amount or value: £409·25.
Additional information required: none

The letter regarding the national savings certificates
he sent to the Director, Savings Certificate and SAYE
Office, Millburngate House, Durham DH99 1NS,
and in this case the completed table said:

*Particulars of asset:*
Name in which held: Herbert G. Blake
Description of asset: savings certificates as listed
on attached schedule
Reference number: BPJ9925
Estimated amount or value: £1,000
Additional information required: none

There were quite a number of national savings certificate books, containing certificates from several of the
various issues of savings certificates that have been
made over the years. Matthew prepared a list on a
separate sheet of paper, setting out the savings certificates individually, specifying the cost of each certificate, the number of units represented by it, the serial
number on the certificate, and the date of its issue,
found by reference to the circular date stamp on it.

Premium savings bonds do not need to have an
official valuation. They retain their face value and no

question of interest arises. They cannot be nominated or transferred to beneficiaries, but may be left in the ERNIE draws for twelve calendar months following the death, and then cashed. The Bond and Stocks Office, Lytham St Annes, Lancashire FY0 1YN, should be notified of the bond holder's death as soon as possible.

Herbert Blake did not have a Giro account. When a Giro account holder dies, his account is administered according to the rules of ordinary banking practice.

Matthew knew that his father-in-law had kept an account at the Minford branch of the Barminster Bank. He found the cheque book, the paying-in book and the bank statements in a drawer in the house. He wrote the letter to the local manager of the branch, with these details:

*Particulars of asset:*
Name in which held: Herbert G. Blake
Description of asset: current account
Reference number:
Estimated amount of value: unknown
Additional information required: please let me know
1. whether Mr Blake kept a deposit account at your branch;
2. whether he kept a deed box at your branch, or otherwise deposited any documents or other property with you.

When assets are held in joint names, it is necessary to fix a value on the share that belonged to the joint owner who died. In the case of a joint bank account, for instance, the executors have to find out the source of the money paid to the credit of the account, as this indicates the proportions in which the credit balance on the date of death was held. If the sole origin of money paid into an account was, for instance, the husband's earnings, it would follow that the whole of the balance in a joint account with his wife was his, and none hers. So on his death the whole balance is liable to estate duty. But if she had died first, nothing need have been included in the valuation of her estate, even though she had power to draw on the account during her life. Where both joint holders contributed from their own money to the joint account, it is necessary to identify payments into the account over a period of years, and to calculate the respective total contributions to the account. The credit balance at the date of death would then be divided between the joint account holders in those proportions. If it is impossible to show who contributed what, or if the items in the account are too numerous or complicated to make it possible to distinguish the sources, the balance is considered to be equally held by its joint holders, and half the balance is liable to estate duty on the death of the first of them to die.

A joint account of husband and wife, incidentally, has the advantage that usually the survivor can continue to draw on the account, even though the other spouse has died. As it can take weeks, even months, to get a grant of probate, this allows the survivor continued access to ready cash. The balance to the credit of a joint account passes automatically to the survivor and so bypasses the will, unless some specific other agreement was made between the joint account holders.

With any assets held jointly—building society accounts, savings bank accounts, and investments for instance—a similar calculation must be made.

Matthew also wrote a letter of enquiry to the Bridstow Insurance Company Ltd. He had found a life assurance policy with that company among the documents in the deed box. It provided for the payment of £3,000 on Herbert Blake's death. Matthew found that it was a 'with profits' policy, which meant that in addition to the £3,000 to be paid to the executors by the insurance company, a further amount would be paid. In the letter to the local branch manager of the insurance company, Matthew gave the following particulars:

*Particulars of asset:*
Name in which held: Herbert George Blake
Description of asset; whole life insurance, issued 14 June 1934
Reference number: policy HPX 9420/34
Estimated amount or value: £3,000
Additional information required: as this policy was 'with profits', please let me know the amount of profits that are payable.

Matthew had now set in train the procedure for valuing the property left by his father-in-law. Even where he knew, or had a fair idea of, the value of an asset, he still wrote to the organisation concerned for a written valuation, in case he should need evidence of the value of any item.

## The house

Matthew now turned his attention to the question of valuing the house. Most people have some idea of the current value of the houses in their locality. It is not essential to obtain a professional valuation from a firm of surveyors and valuers. Whether you have a professional valuation or not, your figure will be checked sooner or later by an official called the district valuer. He is employed by the Inland Revenue, but his job has little to do with taxes as such. He is concerned with the valuation of land, houses, factories, shops, offices and so on, for many official purposes, including deciding rateable values. He is an expert on valuation, so there is no point in trying to understate the value of a house. On the other hand, you may as well put down your lowest estimate of value: the district valuer will query your figure later on if it is too low, but perhaps not if it is on the high side.

Matthew estimated the value of The Firs at £18,000. It is possible, where a house is not going to be sold, and where the total estate will be more than £15,000, to agree a value for the house with the district valuer before applying for probate. As Mrs Blake had not yet decided whether to keep or sell the house, Matthew did not seek the prior agreement of the district valuer to a figure.

Whenever a house is held in the joint names of a husband and wife, the value of the husband's share has to be decided when he dies. There are two different ways in which property may be held jointly: as joint tenants or as tenants in common. Where husband and wife own a house as joint tenants, the share of the first to die passes to the survivor automatically on death. The survivor of joint tenants acquires the other half-share, in fact, merely by surviving. In the case of tenants in common, however, the share of the first to die forms part of the estate; that share may, of course, pass to the spouse under the will, but that is not the same thing as passing to the spouse automatically, as happens when it is a joint tenancy.

It can make a difference to the value of a share in a jointly held house whether it was held as joint tenants or as tenants in common. That would be the first thing for the executor to find out (from the deeds and documents) in the process of valuing the share in a house, on the death of one of the joint owners. If it was held as tenants in common, the executor will have to know the proportions in which it was held in order to estimate the value of the share of the deceased at the date of death. It is often, but not always, held in equal shares.

The vacant possession value at the date of death is the starting point in calculating the value of the deceased's share of the house for estate duty. Suppose it is the figure of £12,500. In the case of a joint tenancy and tenancy in common held in equal shares, that figure must be divided in two, to allow for the share of only the one who died; this would give a figure of £6,250.

But one has not yet arrived at the true net value of the deceased's share. Because it was only a share in a house, and because the other joint owner still has the right to live there, it follows that the deceased's share must be worth less than precisely half of the full value; the value is inhibited by the very fact that someone can still live there. For estate duty, value means the price a buyer would pay in the open market on the day of death. It is hardly likely that a buyer (if one could be found) would pay as much as half of the vacant possession price for a half share, with a stranger still living in the house.

The result is that the proper value of the half share (in the case of a joint tenancy or a tenancy in common held in equal shares) is half the vacant possession value, less something for the mere fact of it being held jointly. The £6,250 for half the vacant possession value might well be depressed to £5,500 on this account. There is no rigid formula that applies to this aspect of the valuation, and it is very difficult to arrive at a figure because, in practice, shares in joint tenancies in ordinary houses are hardly ever sold. Nevertheless, the expert valuer should be able to decide on a figure. Some valuation officers do not readily accept this basis of the value of the share in a house held by the deceased jointly with someone else, but it is correct.

Finally, account must be taken of any mortgage debt outstanding. Suppose that it is £2,000; then the deceased's share of this debt would normally be half, that is £1,000. The result would be that the value of the deceased's share of the house less the mortgage debt would be £5,500 minus £1,000, that is £4,500.

Matthew, however, was not involved in the problem of valuing a share in a house jointly held, because he knew that the house was in Herbert Blake's name alone. If Matthew had been uncertain whether the house was in Herbert Blake's name alone or a joint ownership and there was no declaration of trust or other evidence of joint ownership among Herbert Blake's documents, he would now have enquired of the building society which held the title deeds.

There was a mortgage on the house, on which there was about £800 to be paid, according to a statement from the building society which Matthew had found in Herbert Blake's papers. The statement gave the position as it was on the previous 31 December, and it would be necessary, Matthew knew, to obtain an exact figure showing the position at the date of his father-in-law's death. He wrote this letter to the building society:

14 Twintree Avenue,
Minford, Surrey.
17 May 1972.

Dear Sir,

*Herbert George Blake deceased*

I am an executor of the will of the late Herbert George Blake, who died on 12 May 1972; my co-executor is his widow, Mrs Mary Josephine Blake.

Mr Blake owned the house where he lived: The Firs, Willow Lane, Minford, on which he had a mortgage with your society. The reference number is BM492. Please let me know exactly how much was outstanding on the mortgage at the date of death, including interest due up to that date.

I do not know yet whether the mortgage will be paid off when the grant of probate has been obtained.

I do not appear to have any record of the date on which the mortgage was made. Please let me know this.

Yours faithfully,
Matthew J. Seaton.

The Manager
Minford Building Society
Great Winchester Street
Minford, Surrey.

There had, for obvious reasons, been little discussion so far about whether Mrs Blake would continue to live in the house, or whether it would be sold. For the time being she was staying with Matthew and Emma, and the house was closed up. What was to happen eventually could be decided later on.

*Stocks and shares*

Matthew next turned his attention to the question of finding out the value of another item which made up his father-in-law's property: the stocks and shares.

In the deed box, together with the will, Matthew had found the stock and share certificates for the various holdings. This was what he found:

£550 ordinary stock in ICI Ltd
£1,390 8 per cent preference stock in Unilever Ltd
£680 ordinary stock in The Metal Box Co Ltd
£250 ordinary stock in Wilkinson Sword Ltd
890 ordinary 5s. shares in Shell Transport and Trading Co Ltd
1,460 ordinary 5s. shares in Courtaulds Ltd
£2,355 Norwich Corporation 5 per cent Redeemable Stock (1980)

Matthew had already made a rough calculation of what those items were worth on the date of death, by looking up the closing prices in the paper. Now it became necessary to work it out exactly, and in accordance with the accepted formula for valuing shares for estate duty. This formula applies to stocks and shares which are bought and sold on the London Stock Exchange, and which are therefore quoted there. The shares of all the well known large companies, and a great number of others as well, are quoted on the London Stock Exchange, as are war stock and numerous other government securities and similar investments, but not defence bonds. On any particular day, there are sales of shares in nearly all the big concerns, and the prices often vary, depending on the prevailing circumstances. As a result there is, for any particular day, a range of prices at which shares in any one company will have been sold. The closing price, which is the prevailing price of the share at the time in the afternoon when the stock exchange closed for the day, may differ from the highest and lowest price at which the shares were quoted on that day.

To work out the value which is officially recognised for probate purposes, it is necessary to know the quotations on the day of the deceased's death. This is not the same thing as the closing price, which is the price which is generally found in the financial columns of the newspapers. The Stock Exchange Official List, a daily publication, gives the required figures in a concise way. If the death was at the weekend, quotations for the friday or for the monday may be used.

Not many people have ready access to the Stock Exchange Daily Official List. A very large branch of a bank may take it; but if you telephone your bank manager, quoting the securities you wish to value, he will be able to find out and let you know the two prices for each share for the date of the death in question. If there is a long list, it is probably better to write to the bank. Alternatively, a stockbroker would be able to provide this information quite easily, either on the telephone in the case of a few quotations, or by letter if there are more.

Matthew decided to buy a copy of the Stock Exchange Official List for 12 May, to make the valuation. He wrote to 'Stock Exchange Official List De-

*. . . the formula is this . . .*

partment', 26 Austin Friars, London EC4N 2EU, enclosing £1·85. The list, which was a 32-page newspaper, came four days later. He found that five of the companies in which he was interested were quoted in the section of the Daily List headed: 'Commercial and Industrial'; the Shell shares were classified as being 'Oils', and Norwich Corporation was listed under Corporation and County stocks.

In each case, Matthew found two prices quoted. He was then able to adopt the appropriate formula to work out the value of each for probate purposes. The formula is this: take as the figure a price which is one quarter up from the lower to the higher figure. If the two figures are in the quotation column of the Stock Exchange Official List are, for instance 100p and 104p, then you take 101p as the value; if the two prices were 245p and 255p, then you would take 247·5p as the value. The prices quoted in the Official List are often prices for every £1 of stock held, or for every share held; the nominal value of a share may be 20p, 25p, £1, and might be one of many other amounts as well. Certificates issued before February 1971 are in equivalent shilling units—4s., or 5s.

Matthew prepared a complete table showing the share values. It looked like this:

| Amount held £ | Description | Prices quoted p | $\frac{1}{4}$ up from lower p | Value of holding £ |
|---|---|---|---|---|
| 550 | ICI ordinary stock | 255–275 | 260 | 1,430·00 |
| 680 | Metal Box Co Ltd ordinary stock | 380–405 | 386·25 | 2,626·50 |
| 1,390 | Unilever Ltd 8% cum preference stock | 90–100 | 92·5 | 1,285·75 |
| 250 | Wilkinson Sword Ltd ordinary stock in 20p units | 55–65 | 57·5 | 143·75 |
| 890 | Shell Transport & Trading Co Ltd ordinary shares of 25p each | 305–330 | 311·25 | 2,770·12 |
| 1,460 | Courtaulds Ltd ordinary shares | 130–145 | 133·75 | 1,952·75 |
| 2,355 | Norwich Corporation 5 per cent Red. stock (1980) | 83–87 | 84 | 1,978·20 |
| | | | | 12,187·07 |

So the stocks and shares turned out to be worth, on the date of death, £12,187·07.

Matthew had now set about valuing all the securities he had been able to find belonging to his father-in-law on the day of his death. There was not, apparently, any money in unit trusts. Unit trusts have become a ·common feature of the investment scene. To fix a value for these, an executor should write to the managers of the unit trust in question, to obtain a letter stating the value at the date of death.

(Where shares or unit trust holdings are sold within a year of a death occurring after 6 March 1973 for less than the value on the date of death, the total of the gross selling price of all such investments sold within the year can be substituted as the value for calculating estate duty. Adjustment is made by means of a corrective affidavit.)

To value shares not quoted on the Stock Exchange, for example shares in a private company, requires expert help, as a rule. Sometimes the secretary or accountant of the company concerned can state the price at which shares have recently changed hands, and this may be accepted for probate purposes. If not, a detailed and possibly difficult negotiation of value may have to be undertaken and unless the shares are of comparatively small value, it would be worthwhile to get an accountant to handle the matter.

*Pensions*

Amongst the private papers Matthew found a description of the pension scheme operated by his father-in-law's former employers, an engineering company. This was a contributory pension scheme under which he had received a pension for the three years during which he had lived in retirement. From reading the booklet, Matthew gathered that the scheme would now provide a pension to be paid to Mrs Blake for the rest of her life. This pension would be about half of the pension which her husband had been receiving. No other money would be due under the pension scheme, so there was really only one point arising out of the scheme which was strictly relevant to the administration of Herbert Blake's estate: the proportion of the month's pension due up to the date of his death. Matthew wrote this letter to the secretary of the pension fund:

14 Twintree Avenue,
Minford, Surrey.
21 May 1972

Dear Sir,

*Herbert George Blake deceased*

You will be sorry to hear that Mr Herbert Blake of The Firs, Willow Lane, Minford, died on 12 May. He was, as you know, receiving a pension from the fund administered by you, and it would appear, according to the rules of the fund, of which I have a copy, that his widow, Mrs Mary Josephine Blake, will now be entitled to a widow's pension from the fund.

Mrs Blake is one of the executors of his will, and I am the other. Please let me know the amount of Mr Blake's pension due up to the date of his death, and let me know the amount of pension Mrs Blake will be receiving. If there are any formalities involved in obtaining the pension for Mrs Blake, perhaps you would let me have details, and any forms she must complete.

Finally, please confirm that no capital sum is due to the estate under your pension scheme.

Yours faithfully,
Matthew Seaton.

The Secretary, Staff Pension Scheme,
Minford Engineering Co Ltd,
Minford Lane, Surrey.

Many employers maintain a staff pension scheme; the schemes vary considerably in form and detail.

This one was typical of many, in that it provided for the payment of a pension to a former member of the company's staff, and the pension was calculated according to the contributions made to the pension fund by the company and by the member during the years in which he was employed by the company. This was the pension which Herbert Blake had been receiving during his years of retirement. The scheme then went on to provide for the payment of a further pension to the widow of a pensioner, this being a proportion (in this case half) of the earlier pension. In these circumstances no other payment, such as a capital payment to the executors, was due under the scheme.

Quite often a pension scheme provides that a capital sum should become payable on the death of one of its members; indeed, this could have happened in some circumstances under the scheme to which Herbert Blake had belonged. For instance, if a member were to die while still an employee, that is before retirement, the scheme might provide for the return of the contributions which had been made over the years by the member, and from which he has, in the event, derived no benefit, because he did not survive to collect his pension. This return of contributions would be made in a lump sum, would be part of the deceased's estate, and would have to be declared for estate duty. However, one often finds that where this happens a further payment may be made, this one being under a life assurance scheme which is coupled with the pension scheme. That is to say, the two linked schemes (pension and life assurance) provide between them that, if a member dies in service before retiring, his contributions are returned and, in addition, a capital sum becomes payable. In cases like that, the scheme often provides that the people who administer the scheme may select who is to receive the capital sum. They may pay it all to the widow or they may share it between any number of dependants or pay it to the executors as part of the estate. If they pay it to the widow or to the dependants, the money forms no part of the deceased's estate. As a result, the discretionary payment to a widow or dependant is not subject to estate duty.

Whatever the circumstances, it is probably best, where the deceased belonged to a pension scheme, to get a letter from the secretary of the pension fund to confirm the exact position regarding what the estate (as distinct from a dependant) is entitled to receive under the scheme. Even if it is only the proportion of his pension due for the last few days of his life (as in Herbert Blake's case), a letter should be obtained to provide written confirmation for the purpose of estate duty.

Matthew's father-in-law had also been receiving the state old age pension, or national insurance retirement pension, as it is properly called. Matthew found the pension book and noticed that his father-in-law had not drawn his pension for the four weeks up to the date of his death.

Matthew visited as soon as he could the Minford office of the Department of Health and Social Security. He took with him: his father-in-law's pension book; the death certificate which is specially provided, free of charge, for national insurance purposes by the registrar of births and deaths; and the marriage certificate of Mr and Mrs Blake. There were three distinct matters which had to be discussed at the social security office: the arrears of Mr Blake's retirement pension, the death grant in respect of Mr Blake's death and Mrs Blake's national insurance widow's pension.

Herbert Blake had been receiving the usual state retirement pension, based on his national insurance contributions up to his retirement at the age of 65. Matthew was told that the arrears of pension, as well as the full pension for the week in which death took place, would be paid to the executors. Pensions are paid on a specified day each week, for the week ahead. If a person collects his pension on thursday and then dies on the following monday, his estate would not be liable to refund any part of that week's pension.

Matthew handed in his father-in-law's pension book. The sum due for arrears of pension would be paid to him and to Mrs Blake, as the executors, after probate had been obtained. The arrears of pension formed part of Herbert Blake's estate; it would have to be declared for estate duty and included in the probate papers.

Next, Matthew enquired about the state death grant. This grant depends on a person's national insurance contributions record (or on the date of birth). In Herbert Blake's case there was not likely to be any difficulty or delay in obtaining payment of the full death grant of £30. For some cases where an insufficient number of contributions has been paid or credited in the past, there can be a payment of part of the grant. There is also an appeal machinery, in case of dispute. Matthew completed the claim form to obtain the death grant. The death grant is not liable for estate duty, and does not have to be included as an item of the deceased's property to be declared in the probate papers.

The question of Mrs Blake's widow's pension was the last matter which Matthew discussed. Matthew had filled in the form (BD8) on the back of the certificate which the registrar had given him when he registered the death. On this he applied for Mrs Blake's retirement pension, based on her husband's contributions, to be increased to the rate for a widow, from the date of his death. If she had been under 60 at the time of his death, she would have received an alternative widow's allowance (currently £16·20) for the first 26 weeks after his death and then a pension depending on his national insurance contributions and on her age at the time of his death. The Consumer Publication *What to do when someone dies* gives a detailed account of national insurance grants, allowances and pensions that may be due after a death, and how to obtain them.

Now Matthew wrote to the local inspector of taxes.

> 14 Twintree Avenue,
> Minford, Surrey.
> 24 May 1972.

Dear Sir,

> *Herbert George Blake deceased*

The tax affairs of the above-named have, I believe, been dealt with in your district, under reference B 246537. Mr Blake died on 12 May

1972, and his widow, Mrs Josephhine Blake, of The Firs, Willow Lane, Minford (where the deceased lived) and I are the executors of his will, and we are in the process of applying for a grant of probate.

The only income which Mr Blake was receiving up to the date of his death consisted of: pension from his former employers' pension fund (which was subject to PAYE); his state retirement pension; and dividents from various investments. There may be a small repayment due to Mr Blake in respect of PAYE deducted (and dividends taxed by deduction at the basic rate) for the period up to the date of his death in the current tax year. You will probably be able to calculate this without further information from me, but if there is any information you require for the purpose, please let me know. I shall need to know the amount of the repayment for probate purposes, so I look forward to hearing from you.

Yours faithfully,
Matthew Seaton.

HM Inspector of Taxes
High Street
Minford

Income tax is calculated on a person's total income in the tax year: April to April. PAYE works so that tax is deducted week by week, or month by month, on the assumption that the taxpayer will go on having income throughout the year. If he dies during the year, the PAYE assumptions are upset, because the taxpayer did not live to receive the income throughout the tax year, and often a tax repayment is due. Also, if the taxpayer was not liable for tax at the basic rate, because his income did not reach that level, he may be entitled to a tax repayment if some of his income is taxed at the basic rate before he gets it; dividends from shares fall within this category. It is therefore usual for personal representatives to explain the situation fully to the local inspector of taxes, and if necessary to go and see him about the repayment that may be due because too much income tax was suffered by the deceased during the tax year in which he died. Although tax is only claimed on the amount of income due up to the date of death, tax allowances (such as a married man's personal allowance) are granted for the full year, even if the death took place early in the tax year.

*Contents of house and cash*
The next item requiring valuation was the furniture and effects. This includes furniture in the house, household goods of all kinds, jewellery, clothes, a car and all personal possessions. It is not necessary to prepare a complete list, nor to state the respective values of different kinds of articles; they can all be lumped together.

The make and age of the car are the principal factors which affect its value; its condition is a minor consideration. A study of the prices being asked for secondhand cars by local garages or dealers will give an indication of the value, to within about £20.

The remaining articles are not so easily valued. It is better to put a separate valuation on items of particular value, such as things worth more than about £100, when making a calculation of the total value of the effects. This might apply, for example, to a particular piece of jewellery, or a picture, especially if its value is reasonably well established, because it was recently purchased, for instance, or because it has been valued recently by an expert.

More difficult to fix is a value for the great bulk of the household furniture and effects. How do you decide what the tables, chairs, beds, linen, cups and saucers, carpets, TV set, clothes and all the rest of it are actually worth? You have to decide what price they would get if sold on the day of death. This means in practice what they would fetch at an auction. Of course, the secondhand value of the great majority of items is considerably less than the cost when new. For estate duty, you do not consider the cost of replacement, but the price they would fetch, if sold secondhand. In this respect, there is a parallel with insurance. If all the furniture and effects are destroyed in a fire, say, an ordinary insurance policy does not pay what it costs to replace them, but just their value on the day of the fire. It is the same in the case of valuation for estate duty. The estate duty office of the Inland Revenue does not expect you to provide an expert's valuation, nor one that is accurate to within a few pounds, but a valuation that is honest and sensible, and says what the executor really thinks the items are worth.

This was Matthew's approach to the problem. He spent a saturday afternoon going round the house with his mother-in-law, discussing what was in the house. Where necessary they discussed when, where, and by whom, various items had been bought, in order to exclude items which belonged to her. Matthew made a few notes as they went along. When they had finished, he totted it all up. It came to more than his first guess. The figure he finally arrived at for the furniture and effects was £1,645, plus £1,420 for the car.

One article needed special consideration: the dishwasher. Matthew found that his father-in-law was buying it on hire purchase, and there were four more monthly payments of £11·55 each to be paid. How should this be dealt with in his valuation of Herbert Blake's property? Strictly speaking, the dishwasher itself was not something which belonged to Herbert Blake; it still belonged to the finance company. What Herbert Blake had owned—and which consequently had passed to the executors—was a right to become the owner of the dishwasher, when the remaining instalments had been paid, together with a right to use the dishwasher in the meantime. But it is not necessary to go through the solemn process of trying to value something so esoteric as a right of this kind. It is sufficient to take a commonsense attitude by valuing the article as if it had been part of what the deceased owned, along with everything else, and then to treat the instalments still to be paid as a debt due from him. This is what Matthew did about the dishwasher. His estimate of its current secondhand value, which he put at £90, was included as part of the £1,645, the value of the furniture and effects. The four outstanding hire purchase instalments of £11·55 each he would include as a debt of £46·20. He ignored the fact that these instalments were not actually due at the date of death, but only over the next four months. Matthew would have applied the same process of valuation if it had been the car, or any other articles, which Herbert Blake had been paying for on hire purchase.

Matthew now considered the simplest asset of them all: cash. In the drawer where the deed box containing the will had been kept, and in one or two other places, Matthew found odd sums of cash. Altogether it came to £18·40.

### Debts

If anyone had owed money to Herbert Blake, Matthew would have included it in the list of property declared for estate duty. Any sums of money which are owed to the deceased count as assets. They are debts due to the estate.

Debts due from the deceased have to be listed, too. Any money which he owes reduces what he owns for the purpose of calculating his total property: the liabilities are deducted from the assets. These debts can

consist of almost anything: rates, fuel bills, telephone account, amounts due on credit cards or credit accounts, hire purchase debts and an overdraft, for example. In addition, the funeral expenses must be deducted.

Herbert Blake had a few debts. Matthew found an unpaid bill for rates, which his father-in-law had perhaps forgotten. There was a telephone account as well, and the hire purchase for the dishwasher. In the course of the first few weeks after his father-in-law's death, Matthew received two more bills, and these he added to the list: a bill for servicing the car, and another for some wines and spirits. Matthew assembled the invoices for these items, and wrote a short note to the companies and organisations who were owed money, explaining that they would be paid soon after probate was granted.

It can happen that a personal representative has real reason to wonder whether all the deceased's debts have come to his notice. For this situation there is a special procedure, which involves advertising for creditors. The personal representative puts an advertisement in the *London Gazette* and the local paper announcing that all claims against the estate have to be made by a date not less than two months ahead. Where this is done in the official way, the personal representative is quite safe in dealing with the estate on the basis of the debts known to him on the date by which claims have to be made, according to the advertisement. If a personal representative does not advertise for creditors in this way, there is always a danger, however slight, that after he has parted with the assets to the beneficiaries, some unknown creditor

appears on the scene and justifiably claims that the
deceased owed him money. If that were to happen,
the personal representative would have to pay the
debt out of his own pocket, if he had not advertised
for creditors. He could probably claim the money
back from the beneficiaries, but even that might be
difficult. Matthew did not consider that the situation
in Herbert Blake's case merited officially advertising
for creditors, as there was no reason to suppose that
Herbert Blake had any debts apart from those about
which Matthew already knew, or for which bills
would come in within the next few weeks.

*Applying for probate forms*
Matthew knew that it would probably be a few weeks
before all the information about valuing the estate
would be complete and before he could proceed to
the next stage: applying for the grant of probate. But
it was not too soon to write for the forms that he
would be needing for his application. Matthew had
received a booklet when he had registered the death,
which contained the addresses of the district registries
of the probate registry, from which forms could be
obtained. He wrote to the Probate Personal Application Department, Principal Registry, Room 111,
South West Wing, Bush House, Strand, London,
WC2B 4QR (telephone: 01-836 7366). He asked for
the forms required to enable him to make a personal
application for a grant of probate. It is possible to
write or telephone for the forms to a local district
probate registry or subregistry; they are in Bangor,
Birmingham, Bodmin, Brighton, Bristol, Carlisle,
Carmarthen, Chester, Exeter, Gloucester, Hull,

Ipswich, Lancaster, Leeds, Leicester, Lincoln, Liverpool, Llandaff, Maidstone, Manchester, Middlesbrough Teesside, Newcastle upon Tyne, Norwich, Nottingham, Oxford, Peterborough, Sheffield, Stoke-on-Trent, Winchester and York.

*Finance for estate duty*

Matthew next considered how to raise the money needed to pay the estate duty. In his first rough calculation he had estimated that the duty would be £1,660. In the light of the way the valuation of the property was proceeding, it seemed likely that his first estimate had been too low. He could see that the estate would in fact come to between £37,000 and £38,000; the duty would be around £2,000. Matthew went to see the manager of the branch of the bank where Herbert Blake had kept his account, the Barminster Bank at Minford. The manager agreed to lend the money to Matthew and Mrs Blake for paying the estate duty. Banks usually do, but charge interest. Matthew knew he would have to allow for fees to the probate registry as well, so the overdraft limit was fixed at £2,500. It was arranged that an account should be immediately opened at that branch in the name of the two executors, and would be known as the executorship account. For the time being the account was to be without funds, but Matthew would be sent a cheque book in the course of a few days. When the time came to pay the duty, Matthew and Mrs Blake would sign a cheque for the necessary amount, and the bank would meet it. When, later on, the grant of probate had been obtained (but not before), the executors would be in a position to transfer the money in Herbert Blake's own account at the bank into the executorship account. This would partly reduce the overdraft obtained to pay the duty. The overdraft would be completely paid off when the insurance monies were received. In the meantime, the executors would have to pay interest on the overdraft, even though at the same branch there was another account which was temporarily untouchable, but which really belonged to the executors as well. Sometimes it is possible to arrange with the bank manager that, until probate is obtained, the two accounts shall be treated as one, so that the amount standing to the credit of the deceased's account may be set against the overdraft on the executorship account. But this cannot always be arranged, and there is no way of insisting that it should. Indeed, there is not even a way of insisting that the bank should provide an overdraft to pay the estate duty.

In theory, the executors are faced with an odd dilemma. On the one hand, no bank or insurance company which holds money belonging to the estate may confidently hand any of it over to the executors until a grant of probate is obtained and produced to them; the probate is the only authority which can allow them to part with the money. On the other hand, the executors cannot obtain a grant of probate until they have actually paid the estate duty, or at least most of it. How can they pay the duty, without being able to get their hands on the wherewithal to pay it? It is curious that there are not more howls of protest at the system.

Where there is no bank account, and so no ready access to a bank overdraft, some other means of rais-

*some means of raising the
necessary funds has to be found*

ing the necessary finance to pay the estate duty has to
be found. If there are funds in the National Savings
Bank, these can be used to pay the estate duty. So
can national savings certificates and premium bonds.
A special system operates between the personal
application department of the probate registry and
the Department for National Savings which enables
this to be done. The executor has to explain the need
to use the national savings monies for paying the duty
when he first visits the probate registry; he will be
given a form stating the amount to be paid, which he
must then send to the Department for National Savings, together with the savings bank account book,
the savings certificates, or the premium bonds. The
Department for National Savings will then send a
cheque for the duty direct to the probate registry, and
the balance of the National savings monies will be
made available to the executors after probate is
obtained.

If the person who died had a Giro account, the
executors may, subject to satisfactory identification,
borrow for the purpose of paying estate duty, so that
a grant of probate may be obtained. The borrowing is
limited to solvent estates and to the amount of the
credit balance in the deceased's account.

*Finalising the valuation*

It was not long before Matthew began to receive letters providing a precise valuation of the assets. He heard from the Department for National Savings about the savings bank account and the savings certificates; he heard from the insurance company that, in addition to the £3,500 policy money, the profits to be paid amounted to £568·97.

The bank manager had handed a letter to Matthew when he went to discuss the estate duty, and this letter stated the exact sum which stood to the credit of Herbert Blake's current account at the bank at the date of death: £193·52. The bank account (not being a joint account) was frozen as soon as the manager had been told of Herbert Blake's death. No further payment would be made out of the account either for cheques signed by Herbert Blake but not presented till after his death, or on banker's orders.

Matthew heard from the local inspector of taxes, who stated that a modest tax repayment was due to the estate because his father-in-law had suffered an over-deduction of income tax on his pension.

Matthew heard from the building society about the mortgage on the house. He was told that the amount outstanding on the mortgate on 12 May 1972 was £768·44. He was also told the date of the mortgage, which he had not been able to find in Herbert Blake's records, but which he would need for the probate papers.

Then he heard from the secretary of the pension fund. There was £22·30 due for the proportion of Herbert Blake's pension for the part of the month of May during which he was alive. No other sum was due to the estate from the pension fund, but as from the date of death, Mrs Blake would be entitled to a pension amounting to £438 a year, to be paid monthly. The secretary sent Matthew a form for Mrs Blake to complete. When she had done so, Matthew returned it with the standard death certificate. This was returned to him in a few days, and at the end of the month Mrs Blake started to receive the pension. This, of course, was in addition to the national insurance widow's pension which Mrs Blake would be drawing through the post office.

Within a month of Herbert Blake's death, Matthew had collected all the necessary information about the estate of his father-in-law. The funeral account, amounting to £112·60 was the final document to arrive. Matthew was now able to complete the forms which would enable him to apply for a grant of probate.

*Filling in probate forms*

Matthew had received the probate forms from the personal application department of the probate registry in London, and it would be with that department at Bush House in London that Matthew would be making all further arrangements. Had he lived in the provinces, he would have obtained the forms from, and would be making all further arrangements with, the nearest district registry of the probate registry. The procedure, after the forms are completed, can vary in minor respects not only between London and the provincial towns, but also between different district registries.

In the past it was usually necessary for the executor to attend personally at the probate registry on two occasions. On the first visit he brought the forms and these were checked. The probate fee and estate duty were assessed, and an appointment was then made for a second visit. Between the two visits, the provisional assessment of duty was checked at the estate duty office and the registry officials prepared the document which the executor, when he made his second visit, would swear to be true.

In the probate registries outside London it is often possible, in straightforward cases, for the matter to be completed with only one visit by the executor. In London a postal system is now in operation which often enables the matter to go through with only one visit by the executor. Instead of bringing in the forms which he has completed, he may send them in by post, and if they are in order, an appointment is made, by post, for him to attend to swear the papers. But one visit will do only if the estate is a comparatively uncomplicated one; and only where the executor has filled in his forms correctly, and where no queries arise on them or on the will.

The forms which Matthew had received by post from the probate registry were these:

form 48: an explanation of the procedure on making a personal application

form 38: a form of instructions for probate

form 44: *Return for estate duty*

form 37A: *Schedule of real and/or leasehold property in the United Kingdom*

form 40: *Statement of stocks and shares.*

*Form 38*

To complete form 38 was quite simple. It contained panels in which Matthew gave the required information. Firstly the form asked at which office the applicant wished to attend. Matthew put London. Next it asked for particulars about the deceased: *full name* (Herbert George Blake), *address* (The Firs, Willow Lane, Minford, Surrey), *place of death* (Minford, Surrey), *date of death* (12 May 1972), *occupation* (retired factory manager), *age* (68), *status* (married).

Next Matthew completed particulars of the applicants, himself and his mother-in-law: *full names* (1) Mary Josephine Blake and (2) Matthew John Seaton; *postal addresses and telephone number* (1) The Firs, Willow Lane, Minford, Surrey and (2) 14 Twintree Avenue, Minford, Surrey, Minford 4974; *occupation* (1) housewife and (2) company secretary; *relationship to deceased* (1) widow and (2) son-in-law.

Some general information was required. *Did the deceased leave a will?* Answer: yes. *If 'yes' and the applicant is not an executor is anyone named in the will under 18?* Answer: no.

The form then had a space for naming, in those cases where it was appropriate, any executors who were not applying for probate, and the reason.

Next, Matthew had to give details of the surviving relatives: widow, 3 sons or daughters 18 or over, 2 grandchildren.

Lastly, there were spaces for information about illegitimate children (where a will is not being proved by an executor).

Matthew found that he did not have to sign form 38. This was because the form is used for the probate registry as the basis for another form, called an oath, which they prepare. The oath contains the same particulars, more or less, as form 38, but the oath expresses them in the stipulated legal language.

### Form 44

The rest of the forms were mainly concerned with providing details of the property which the deceased had left. Form 44 is the main one. It is used as the basis for the preparation by the probate registry of the actual document which the personal representatives will have to swear: the Inland Revenue affidavit. There is space on form 44 to fill in details of each of the assets which comprise the deceased's estate. The form itself contains reasonably clear instructions about what has to be included and how to fill it in. Pages 1 and 2 of form 44 comprise a number of questions which have to be answered YES or NO. The main part of the form begins on page 3, under the heading 'property of the deceased in the United Kingdom', and it is best to turn to that part first.

Matthew had by him all the letters and memoranda which he had obtained about the value of the various assets. Item 1 on page 3 of the form was for British Savings Bonds, National Development Bonds, War Loan and other government securities. Matthew could have found a valuation for War Loan and Savings Bonds in the Stock Exchange Official List; Defence Bonds are worth their face value. As it happened, Herbert Blake had none of these, so there was nothing to fill in there.

Item 2 was for savings certificates. Matthew wrote 'see letter' alongside, as he meant to attach to the form 44 the actual letter from the Department for National Savings showing the value of the savings certificates. The figure he wrote in the column headed 'Principal value at date of death' was £942·50. Matthew kept a note of the main points of the letter from the Department for National Savings, as he would need to know them when it came to cashing the savings certificates after probate had been obtained.

Item 3 was for details of premium bonds. Herbert Blake did not have any, so Matthew left this space on the form blank.

Item 4 on the form said: 'Other Stocks, Shares or Investments including Unit Trusts'. If Herbert Blake had owned just one or two lots of shares, Matthew could have written the details of them on form 44. But there were seven lots of stocks and shares here, and therefore not enough room to give the required particulars of them all. One of the other forms he had been sent was specially designed for providing these details, so Matthew used it.

*Form 40*

A buff-coloured form, form 40 is ruled into columns to enable the necessary data about the stocks and shares to be set out in tabular form. When completed, form 40 looked rather like the valuation which Matthew had prepared for his own benefit. The form was headed 'Statement of Stocks and Shares etc'. The first (and main) column in it asked for a full description of the class of share or stock. In Matthew's case this required the name of the companies or concerns and a description of the types of stock or shares. Quite often companies issue different denominations of stocks and shares, such as '7 per cent Preference Stock', 'Debenture Stock' and others, as well as their ordinary stocks or shares. So it was necessary to specify the type of stock or shares, as well as the name of the company.

The next column asked for the unit of quotation. This meant the unit of the stock or shares, the value of which was quoted on the stock exchange. In the case of stock, the unit of quotation is often £1, but not necessarily so. In the case of shares, the unit of quotation is one share, as a rule.

The next column in form 40 was headed 'Holding—No. of Shares or amount of Stock'. This asked for the quantity which the deceased had held of the investment concerned, measured in terms of so much of the unit of quotation, referred to in the previous column.

The next column asked for the market price at date of death. This is where the formula of the 'one quarter up' applies. Having found the quotations in the Stock Exchange Official List, Matthew entered on the form the figure one quarter up from the lower price, as this was the recognised market value for the purpose of estate duty.

The next column was headed: 'Source of Market Price if other than London Stock Exchange Official List for date of death'. Some shares are quoted on provincial stock exchanges. Shares in a private company (a family business, for example) are also not quoted on the London Stock Exchange. Where this happens, it is sometimes difficult to establish an authoritative valuation of the shares, and professional assistance in arriving at an acceptable valuation is likely to be needed. In the normal case, such as Herbert Blake's, the column does not apply and is left blank.

The last column to be completed on form 40 asked for the principal value at date of death. This was arrived at by multiplying the number of shares or the amount of stock by the market price at date of death.

Matthew completed form 40 with particulars of the seven holdings of stocks and shares which Herbert Blake had owned. The total value came to £12,187·07 and this was the figure which he entered as item 4 on form 44, for 'Other stocks, shares and investments'.

*Form 44 again*

He wrote the words 'See form 40' alongside item 4, to indicate where full details could be found of how the £12,188·70 was made up.

The fifth item to be listed on form 44 was cash. Matthew had collected and counted it, and it had come to £18·40, so that was the figure he entered. He had not considered it necessary to pay the actual notes and coins he had found belonging to his father-in-law into the executorship bank account. It was quite in order to hand the cash to Mrs Blake, for her own immediate needs.

Item 6 on form 44 was: 'Cash at Bank, namely at . . .'. Matthew wrote in: 'Barminster Bank, Minford' and filled in the amount—£193·52—in the figures column.

The next item was: 'Money at SAVINGS BANKS or in BUILDING, CO-OPERATIVE or FRIENDLY SOCIETIES, including interest to date of death'. In

Herbert Blake's case there was merely the money in the National Savings Bank, so that was what Matthew wrote on the form and the amount including the interest on the money which had accrued up to the date of death: £389·20. Had there been any other assets of that category, money in a building society, for instance, a friendly society, or any other savings bank, the procedure would have been the same.

Item 8 was for insurance policies. Where the form asked for the name of the company, Matthew filled in 'Bridstow Insurance Co Ltd', and the amount to be shown in the figures column was the amount to be paid in respect of the policy including bonuses. The letter from the insurance company had stated this amount: £4,068·97.

Item 9 was intended also for insurance policies, but this time for policies taken out by the deceased on someone else's life: someone who was still alive. Occasionally, a woman takes out a policy on the life of her husband, because she has a vital financial interest on his continued ability to earn money; an employer may insure against the death of a crucial employee, such as a managing director. In these and other ways, one sometimes finds a case of one person insuring someone else's life. Where this happens, the policy counts as an asset in the estate of the person who took out the policy, and the value to be shown is the surrender value at the date of death. This is something which the insurance company would give in a letter to the executors. Herbert Blake had no such policies.

Item 10 on form 44 referred to 'household and personal goods'. Matthew had already carefully valued them. The value of the car was £1,420 and £1,645 was the value of the remaining items. He put the figure of £3,065 in the figures column of the form alongside item 10 without explanation; none was needed.

Item 11 asked for 'amounts due from employers'. The proportion of Herbert Blake's pension from his former employer's pension fund after the date of his death amounted to £22·30. Matthew entered this amount on the form.

Item 12, 'other assets', was an omnibus item, the place to fill in details of almost anything not covered elsewhere. Matthew included two items here: the arrears of the state retirement pension, amounting to £32; and the tax refund due from the Inland Revenue, amounting to £9·23. He completed the item on the form with these bare details, and did not add any particulars, nor include supporting evidence.

Item 13 covered post-war credits. Herbert Blake had received repayment of these some years before his death. Matthew therefore left blank item 13 on the form.

Item 14 covered a civil servant's gratuity, the capital sum paid to permanent civil servants on retirement, or to their estates if they die in service. Herbert Blake had not been a civil servant, so there was nothing to fill in there.

Item 15 only applies where the deceased owned a business; Herbert Blake did not, and Matthew ignored the item.

Item 16 was the one for the house. It asked about 'Freehold and leasehold property situated at . . .' Matthew completed the address of the house which

Herbert Blake had owned and lived in: The Firs, Willow Lane, Minford. Alongside, he wrote his estimate of the value of the house: £18,000. He turned his attention to form 37A, referred to in item 16. It was headed: SCHEDULE OF REAL AND/OR LEASEHOLD PROPERTY IN THE UNITED KINGDOM.

*Form 37A*

The form was designed to cover a great variety of properties, not only houses. Columns 4, 5, 6, 7 applied to property that was let and as that did not apply to Matthew's case, he left them blank. Column 2 asked for a description of the property, and Matthew wrote its postal address. Column 3 asked what the 'tenure' was; the answer was: freehold. If the property had been of leasehold tenure, the number of unexpired years of the lease would also have had to be shown in column 3.

There was also a reference to restrictive covenants, which sometimes affect the value of the property, for example, by preventing it being used for commercial purposes. If, for example, other houses in the road had been turned into offices and the local authority's development plan allowed commercial use of these houses, the value of a house might be enhanced by the possibility of it being turned into offices. The argument for a higher value would be much less strong, if there were restrictive covenants preventing commercial use. This does not often apply to ordinary houses, and did not apply to The Firs. Matthew therefore left the column blank.

The important question came in column 8: 'Principal value . . .' which meant the capital value on the open market at the date of death. This was where Matthew filled in the figure £18,000. The outstanding amount of the mortgage debt is treated separately as a debt for estate duty purposes, rather than an amount by which the value of the property is reduced. Only property which has a capital value has to be included for estate duty. A tenancy of a house or flat normally has no capital value and nothing need be said about it in the probate forms.

Column 9 covered farms and factories. Matthew left it blank.

At the bottom of the form were three spaces for details of timber, sales (of the house, for instance) and tithe redemption annuity. None of them applied to Matthew's case, so he ignored them. He wrote the name of the deceased and his date of death at the bottom of the form, and form 37A was complete.

### Form 44 again

Pages 1 and 2 of the form 44 were devoted to further items of property which have to be included for probate purposes where they exist. None of them applied to Herbert Blake's estate. Item 1 was about settled property. A settlement is an arrangement whereby one person transfers some of his property (generally

some investments) during his lifetime to trustees who are directed to pay the income from the investments to one person for a period, often for that person's life, and then to divide up the capital among others. Wealthy people often make a settlement on the marriage of one of their children, when it is called a marriage settlement. A similar sort of disposition of property can also be made in a person's will, but then it operates only after the death of the person who makes it. Herbert Blake had not been entitled to an interest under a settlement during his lifetime. Matthew therefore deleted the YES, leaving NO.

Item 2 on page 1 was about accumulations. This is something that could have arisen under a settlement if Herbert Blake had made one. Matthew felt it was unlikely that his father-in-law had indulged in anything so sophisticated as making a settlement that would accumulate income and cease on his death, and therefore, as with item 1, the answer was NO.

Item 3 was about gifts made by the deceased within seven years of his death. (Gifts to any recipient amounting to more than £500 are counted as part of the estate and may be liable to estate duty.) All gifts, irrespective of value, have to be shown and details of the date, value, to whom given and address, has to be stated. Wedding presents do not usually count as a gift, however hefty they may be. The personal representatives must enquire among those who are most likely to have received gifts, and only if everyone says 'no' should they answer NO on form 44, as Matthew did.

In this connection, it is not sufficient, furthermore, to give away your house if you make it a condition that you be allowed to live in the house for the rest of your life. Such an arrangement would fail to avoid liability for estate duty on the house, even though you died more than seven years after the gift.

Item 4 was about policies of assurance. There are all sorts of insurance policies that can be taken out, apart from ordinary life or endowment policies, particulars of which would already have been shown in item 8 on page 3 of form 44. For example, some policies provide that the money shall be paid to a named relative, such as a daughter, rather than form part of the deceased's estate. Item 4 was concerned with any such policies on which the deceased had paid a premium within the last seven years. Matthew said: NO.

Item 5 was about nominations, that is property of any kind nominated by the deceased during his lifetime in favour of any person. For example, savings bank accounts, savings certificates and friendly society accounts can be nominated in this way. The effect is similar to leaving them by will to the person nominated, but they do not form part of the deceased's estate, and so do not pass through the hands of the personal representatives. Instead, they pass direct to the person to whom they are nominated. Nevertheless, they have to be declared for the purposes of estate duty, and details must be included in item 5. There being none in Herbert Blake's case, Matthew replied: NO.

Item 6 on form 44 was headed: 'Superannuation benefits'. It asked whether any sum of money or annuity became payable on his death to any person under a superannuation scheme. In Herbert Blake's

E

case, the answer to this was: yes. Under the staff pension scheme, a pension now became payable to his widow. Although this was not, in the particular circumstances, an item which gave rise to liability to estate duty, Matthew attached a copy of the letter from the secretary of the staff pension scheme maintained by Minford Engineering Co Ltd.

Item 7 asked whether there was any property held jointly. Had there been a house held jointly, or a joint bank account, the answer would have been: yes. The purpose of the question, broadly speaking, was to find out the source of funds used to acquire the joint property; to determine what proportion of the purchase money actually came from the deceased's resources. This is often crucial in fixing the extent of estate duty liability on the joint property.

In Matthew's case, completing item 7 on form 36 was easy. There was no jointly held property in Herbert Blake's case, so Matthew simply replied: NO.

Page 6 (Account 2) of form 44 was for property which is physically outside the United Kingdom. A villa in Spain would have had to be included there; so would an interest in a business which was carried on abroad.

At the bottom of page 6 was a space for the signatures of the applicants, in this case Mrs Blake and Matthew.

Page 5 of form 44 was for details of debts. Matthew had earlier assembled the bills which he had been able to find, for rates, telephone, wines and spirits, car service, and hire purchase on the dishwasher. In the left-hand column Matthew filled in particulars in each case of who was owed the money in the next column—under 'Description of debt'—he stated what each was for: general rates, telephone and so on; in the third column he filled in the amount of each debt. Matthew totalled the debts, and they came to £103·60. In the middle of the page was a space for details of the funeral expenses. Matthew inserted the name of the funeral directors and the amount of their bill—£112·60. There was then a space for the total of the debts and the funeral expenses, which in this case was £216·20.

At the bottom of the page was the space for details of a mortgage. This applied in Herbert Blake's case, and Matthew filled in the details of the mortgage with the Minford Building Society, from whom he had obtained particulars. In the column alongside, he stated the amount of money which was outstanding at the date of death: £768·44.

Where a property is held jointly, the amount to be included as a debt is the deceased's share of the mortgage (normally half in the case of a joint tenancy).

Finally, the form asked for details of any business debt. This only applies where the deceased carried on a business himself. Matthew left the column blank.

### Sending off the forms

Matthew went carefully through the completed forms with Mrs Blake, and explained each item to her, to be sure that she understood it and that it was accurately completed. She did and each was. Of the three forms which Matthew had completed, only form 44 needed to be signed.

Matthew made a copy of Herbert Blake's will. He would be posting the original to the probate registry, and although the letter would be registered, he thought that the original will should not be sent without his first taking a copy. Then he bundled into the large envelope, which had come with the forms, these documents: the will, death certificate, form 38, form 44, form 37A and form 40. To form 44 he attached the original letter from the Department for National Savings about the savings certificates and a copy of the letter from the secretary of Herbert Blake's firm's pension fund. He enclosed a short covering letter listing the enclosures, and sent it by registered post to the personal application department of the probate registry in London.

If there had been any queries in the forms, Matthew would probably have received a letter from the registry asking him to attend there. The difficulties would then have been cleared, and an appointment subsequently made for Mrs Blake and him to go to the registry to swear the papers. As it happened, there were no queries, and ten days after sending the forms, Matthew received a form from the registry, which asked him and Mrs Blake to come to Bush House at a stated time on a particular day, 2.30 p.m. on 4 July.

*Estate duty and fees*
On the back of the form which he received a few days later were particulars of what would have to be paid by way of estate duty and probate registry fee. The provisional estimate of the estate duty was £2,138·14.

This £2,138·14 was the duty on the amount of the net estate, which is the value of the assets less the debts (including the mortgage) and the funeral expenses, plus interest at 3 per cent per annum from the date of death to the date of payment. Interest is paid on everything except houses and land (freehold or leasehold) and some unquoted shares. Payment of the proportion of estate duty for these can be delayed by up to one year and no interest becomes due during that year, unless the property is sold. Furthermore, the duty on a house can be paid off over eight years by instalments. When a freehold house is not left to the residuary legatee, the person who gets it must bear the estate duty for the house.

The system of charging estate duty for the estates of people who died after 21 March 1972 is as follows. The first £15,000 of the net estate is exempt from duty. That is to say you pay duty only on any excess over £15,000. In addition, up to £15,000 of property given to the deceased's widow or widower is free of estate duty. (Also, up to £50,000 given to charities is free of estate duty.) In a case such as Herbert Blake's, therefore, the first £30,000 of his estate was free of duty.

Above £15,000 (£30,000 where the widow or widower gets £15,000) the duty works in slices.

Assuming that the property is given to the widow, estate duty is at the rate of 25 per cent on the excess over £30,000, up to £35,000. This means that on a net estate of £34,000 where everything goes to the widow, the duty comes to £1,000, which is 25 per cent of the difference between £30,000 and £34,000. On a net estate of £35,000 duty is £1,250 (25 per cent of £5,000). On the slice of the net estate which lies between £35,000 and £45,000 the rate of duty is

30 per cent. This means that, for example, on a net estate of £42,000 left to the widow, the duty comes to £3,350 (made up of £1,250 the duty on £35,000 plus £2,100 the 30 per cent duty on the £7,000 by which the net estate exceeds £35,000). In this way the rate of estate duty increases by slices until at the top rate the duty on the excess of estates over £500,000 is 75 per cent.

Where there is no widow or widower, estate duty starts at £15,000 and is charged at 25 per cent on the net estate between £15,000 and £20,000; at 30 per cent between £20,000 and £30,000 and so on.

Where the widow or widower gets less than £15,000 but the net estate is above that figure, the amount left to her or him is exempt and on top of that the first £15,000 of the rest of the estate is exempt.

As well as estate duty, there would be probate fees to pay. These are charges made by the probate registry for dealing with the papers and issuing the grant of probate. They fall into two parts. There is the normal probate fee, which is paid in all cases, including those where a solicitor takes out the grant. Then there is an additional fee which has to be paid where the grant is taken out without a solicitor through the personal application department. It covers the extra work involved in the registry where the personal representatives are not legally represented. Both of these fees are calculated on the amount of the net estate, as declared for the purpose of estate duty. In Herbert Blake's case, they came to £40 and £29 respectively, so the total probate fees to be paid were £69. (If a solicitor had dealt with the estate of Herbert Blake and charged according to the Law Society's recommended scale, the fee would have been over £1,000.)

This is how the £2,138·14 was arrived at:

|  | £ | £ |
|---|---|---|
| Value of assets other than house | 20,928·22 | |
| Debts: ordinary £103·60 | | |
| funeral £112·60 | | |
| | 216·20 | |
| Net personal estate | | 20,712·02 |
| Value of house | 18,000·00 | |
| Mortgage debt | 768·44 | |
| Net real estate | | 17,231·56 |
| Total net estate | | £37,943·58 |

Estate duty payable on £7,943·58
25 per cent on £5,000 (£1,250)
plus 30 per cent on £2,943·58
(£883·07)            £2,133·07

Proportion of £2,133·07 attributable to net personal estate of £20,712·02 is £1,164·37
Interest at 3 per cent on £1,164·37 for 53 days is      5·07

Total duty and interest     £2,138·14

Here are some examples of probate fees on personal application for net estates up to £40,000.

| net estate | total probate fees on personal application |
|---|---|
| £ | £ |
| 4,500 | 9 |
| 12,000 | 27 |
| 17,000 | 37 |
| 20,000 | 40 |
| 25,000 | 47·50 |
| 30,000 | 55 |
| 32,000 | 61 |
| 35,000 | 62·50 |
| 37,943·58 | 69 |
| 40,000 | 70 |

Estate duty and the probate fees must be paid when the personal representatives go to the registry to swear the papers. Payment can be made in cash, by cheque, banker's draft or money order. Separate cheques are required for the duty and the probate fee. Matthew drew two cheques on the executorship account, which he and Mrs Blake had recently opened at the bank. One was for £2,138·14, and was for estate duty; the other was for £69 and was for the probate fees. Matthew had already arranged with the bank manager for a temporary overdraft to meet these expenses.

*Swearing the papers*

On the day appointed for their interview at the probate registry, Mrs Blake and Matthew went to London, where they took a bus to the Aldwych and found the door of the south-west wing of Bush House. Matthew took with him to the probate registry the file with all the papers he had accumulated in connection with Herbert Blake's estate so that he could check the accuracy of the forms they would be asked to swear as being correct. They made their way to room 111 on the first floor, and there handed in the form which they had been sent. The first thing to do was to pay the estate duty and the probate fees. Matthew produced the two cheques to the cashier in room 111, who checked them with the form and the records.

The information which Matthew had supplied on the forms had now been translated on to formal printed legal documents, the executor's oath and affidavit. In the blanks were various details of the life, death and family of Herbert Blake and his property. Mrs Blake and Matthew carefully went through each part of the oath and affidavit which seemed to tally exactly with the information which Matthew had supplied. A few minutes later they were asked to take the forms to the room of the commissioner who would deal with their case. He explained that they ought to be completely satisfied that the details in the forms were true in every respect before signing. As personal representatives, theirs was the responsibility that everything was completely and truthfully stated.

Satisfied that everything was in order, both Matthew and Mrs Blake signed the oath and the Inland Revenue affidavit in the space provided at the end of each. They also signed the original will, as indicated to them by the commissioner; the oath contained a clause identifying the will as Herbert Blake's. Then, at the request of the commissioner, each of them stood up in turn, held up a copy of the new testament in the right hand and repeated aloud these words after the commissioner: 'I swear by almighty God that this is my name and handwriting, and that the contents of these my affidavits are true.' As each said the words '. . . name and handwriting' the commissioner pointed to their signatures on the oath and the affidavit.

Instead of swearing on the bible, a personal representative who has grounds for objecting to taking an oath, can affirm by holding up his right hand and saying 'I solemnly and sincerely affirm that this . . .'

The commissioner signed beneath each of their signatures and signed the will below where they had signed it. Their business at the probate registry was now done, except for ordering three photocopies of the grant of probate, when it was issued. When this was done, they left Bush House.

*Letters of administration*
If Herbert Blake had left no will, Mrs Blake would have been applying for a grant of letters of administration, instead of probate; likewise, if he had left a will but it had appointed no executors, or if the executors appointed in the will did not apply for probate. In those cases the grant would have been called 'letters of administration with will annexed'. When letters of administration are being sought, the administrators may have to provide a guarantee of their integrity.

This is only likely to happen where the beneficiaries are under age or mentally disabled. The guarantee is provided by an insurance company or by individuals who undertake to make good—up to the gross value of the estate—any deficiency caused by the administrators failing in their duties.

## The grant

It takes up to three weeks, from when the papers are sworn, for the grant of probate or letters of administration to be issued. If it is not through in three weeks, the personal representatives should get in touch with the probate registry to find out the cause of the delay. A technicality may be holding things up, so that a further visit to the registry may be necessary. In Matthew's case there was no hitch. Fourteen days after their visit to Bush House the grant of probate arrived through the post.

It was signed by a registrar of the probate registry, and the essence of it read as follows '. . . the last Will and Testament (a copy of which is hereunto annexed) of the said deceased was proved and registered in the Principal Probate Registry of the High Court of Justice and that Administration of all the estate which by law devolves to and vests in the personal representative of the said deceased was granted by the aforesaid Court to Mary Josephine Blake and Matthew John Seaton'.

Attached to the probate was a photocopy of the will, the original will being kept at Somerset House in London. Two leaflets were enclosed; one very briefly explained the procedure for collecting in the estate and urged Mrs Blake and Matthew to obtain legal advice in the event of any dispute or difficulty. The other explained how to get legal advice under the legal aid scheme.

The grant was what they had been striving for. It confirmed that they were entitled to deal with Herbert Blake's property, to pay his debts, and then to distribute the property in accordance with his will. It is a public document in the sense that anybody, including any beneficiary, and even the press, can obtain a copy of it or of the will from Somerset House for a small fee.

When he had the probate, Matthew lost no time in proceeding with the administration. Enclosed with the probate were the three photocopies of it for which he had asked. In this way it was possible to proceed with the administration more quickly. Instead of having to send the probate in turn to each outfit requiring to see it, it was possible to send it to the bank, the insurance company, the Department of National Savings and the inspector of taxes, for instance, all on the same day, by sending the original to one of them, and photocopies to the remainder.

Matthew wrote a similar letter to all those who had to see the probate or a photocopy of it:

> 14 Twintree Avenue
> Minford, Surrey.

Dear Sir,

> *Herbert George Blake deceased*
> I enclose the probate of the will of the above for registration with you. Please return it to me when this has been done, and send me what is due to the estate as described in your letter to me of . . .

> Yours faithfully,
> Matthew Seaton.

He sent this letter to the insurance company, the secretary of the firm's pension scheme, the Department of Health and Social Security (about the arrears of retirement pension and the death grant) and the inspector of taxes (about the tax refund), and to the Department for National Savings, enclosing the withdrawal form signed by himself and Mrs Blake.

To the bank manager Matthew wrote the following letter:

> 14 Twintree Avenue,
> Minford, Surrey.
> 22 July 1972.

Dear Sir,

### Herbert George Blake deceased

I now enclose the probate of the will and shall be glad if you will return it to me when you have recorded it. Will you please now close the deceased's current account at your branch and transfer the money in it to the executorship account which my co-executor (Mrs Blake) and I recently opened at your branch.

I am now collecting the rest of the assets and this should result in our being able to pay off the overdraft on the executorship account in the near future.

> Yours faithfully,
> Matthew Seaton.

There was £193·52 in Herbert Blake's current account when he died, and the cheques for the estate duty and the probate fees had given rise to an overdraft amounting to £2,207·14 on the executorship account. This was now reduced to £2,013·62 by the funds from the deceased's own bank account. Banks as a rule do not allow the credit on the deceased's bank account to be treated as available for a beneficiary's use until probate is obtained. As a result, a son for instance may be faced with paying overdraft interest to a bank while at the same time there is money available in the same bank which stands to the credit of an account which is beneficially his.

Within a few days the money arrived from the Department for National Savings and £4,068·97 from the insurance company. Not long after, the proceeds of the savings bank account and the savings certificates arrived from the Department for National Savings.

When the probate, or a copy of it, was returned by one of the organisations which owed money to the estate, Matthew sent if off to any others who had not yet seen it. All who had to pay money to the executors required to see it, and enter details of it in their records; this is often referred to as 'registering the probate'. They usually put their stamp on the back of the probate. Soon all the money which was to be paid to the estate had been received by Matthew and paid into the executorship account at the bank. The overdraft, and the interest on it, was paid off, and the account stood healthily in credit.

Matthew now paid the debts: the rates, the phone, garage, and wines and spirits bills. He also paid the funeral bill.

*Hire purchase on the dishwasher*
His next task was to deal with the hire purchase on

the dishwasher. He had written to the finance company soon after his father-in-law's death to explain that no instalments could be paid until after the grant of probate was obtained. He now decided that the easiest thing to do was to pay all the outstanding instalments in one. Rather than go through the paraphernalia of continuing the hire purchase agreement in the name of Mrs Blake, he sent to the finance company a cheque for what was outstanding—£46·20—plus £1 for the actual purchase of the machine. He got a receipt, and there was no further difficulty. Sometimes a hire purchase company gives a rebate when a hire purchase debt is paid off early in this way.

He could, if he had preferred, have arranged for the agreement to be continued in Mrs Blake's name, or in the name of the executors, in which case he would still have paid the instalments out of the estate.

*Estate duty clearance*
Matthew heard from the district valuer for Minford who considered that Matthew's figure of £18,000 for The Firs was too low. After some bargaining, they agreed that the figure should be £19,000. Matthew then wrote to the estate duty office in London:

14 Twintree Avenue,
Minford, Surrey.
12 August 1972.

Dear Sir,

*Herbert George Blake deceased
date of death 12 May 1972*
I refer to the Inland Revenue affidavit in

regard to this estate and to the provisional payment of estate duty amounting to £2,138·14.

The only item which requires amendment is the value of the house, which was sworn at the sum of £18,000. Following a discussion with the district valuer, this figure has been revised to £19,000. Please let me have your assessment for the additional duty which, according to my calculation, should be £300 (£1,000 at 30 per cent). I will then send you a cheque, after which please let me have your clearance certificate.

Yours faithfully,

The Controller                    Matthew Seaton.
Estate Duty Office
Rockley Road
London W14 0DF.

When there is no provisional agreement with the district valuer about the value of a house, the first contact with him is after probate has been obtained. Where this happens, the value of the house as finally agreed with the district valuer may be higher than the value included in the Inland Revenue affidavit. This results in a further payment of duty having to be made at this stage.

Additional duty would also become due at this stage if the executors discovered some asset of which they had no knowledge when the papers were sworn. They may, for instance, find that the deceased had a deposit account at a bank which was different from the bank where he kept his current account. Where this happens, details have to be given to the estate duty office, and it may be necessary to swear a further affidavit, known as a corrective affidavit. Occaionally, if an asset was mistakenly overestimated in value, or if a new debt appears, there may be some duty to be returned to the personal representatives. One way or another, when the matter is brought to a conclusion, the estate duty office will, when asked, issue to the personal representatives a clearance certificate. This is in effect an acknowledgment that the estate duty office is satisfied, on the basis of the information disclosed, that what has been paid is all the estate duty that will be due. It is only when they have this clearance certificate that the personal representative can safely proceed to distribute the money they have in hand to those entitled to it, secure in the knowledge that the estate duty office will not later be claiming more duty.

In Herbert Blake's case there was no difficulty. Matthew received the assessment, sent the £300 and obtained the clearance certificate, and had nothing further to worry about regarding estate duty.

## Transfer of the house

Matthew discussed with his mother-in-law the question of the house. She had decided that she did not want to sell the house yet, and would shortly return from Matthew and Emma's house—where she had been staying since her husband died—to live in her old home. So it was decided that the executors should transfer the house to Mrs Blake rather than sell it. They discussed the mortgage, and decided that the sensible thing to do was to pay it off out of the money in hand and then to transfer the house into Mrs Blake's name alone, with no further bother for her about the mortgage. So Matthew wrote to the building society:

14 Twintree Avenue,
Minford, Surrey.
22 August 1972.

Dear Sir,

*Herbert George Blake deceased*
*The Firs, Willow Lane, Minford*

I now enclose the probate for registration and return.

The executors have decided to pay off the mortgage with your society as soon as this can be arranged, so please take this letter as formal notice to you of their intention to do this.

Please let me know how much is required to redeem the mortgage as at 31 August. I shall then arrange to let you have a cheque for that amount on that day. You will then, no doubt, forward the deeds of the house to me, together with the official receipt of the society acknowledging that the mortgage has been paid off.

On the question of insurance, we wish to continue the existing policy, but to have it transferred to the name of Mrs Blake, and to take the opportunity of increasing the cover to the present value of the house, £19,000. Will you please arrange this, or put me in touch with the insurance company so that I can do so.

Yours faithfully,

Matthew Seaton.

The Manager
Minford Building Society
Great Winchester Street
Minford, Surrey.

*—registered*

The title to the house was a registered one. It was not strictly accurate therefore of Matthew to have spoken of the deeds of the house, although it is common practice in the legal profession to do so. He really meant the charge certificate, which the building society held as part of its security for the money it had lent. When a house has a registered title, and a mortgage on it is completely paid off, the building society hands back the charge certificate to the owner, together with an official acknowledgment that the money due under the mortgage had been paid. This acknowledgment is usually on a special Land Registry form, known as form 53. The owner then sends the charge certificate, together with form 53, to the Land Registry. A week or so later he receives from the registry the land certificate, which is substantially the same as the charge certificate, but with the very important difference of having had the details of the mortgage officially crossed out. In this way the owner obtains formal proof of his ownership, free from any mention of a mortgage.

Herbert Blake was currently registered at the Land Registry as being the owner—or registered proprietor, to use the official expression—of 'The Firs', Willow Lane, Minford. It would be necessary to prove that the executors now replaced him, and to do that the probate would have to be registered with the Land Registry. And, in this case, there was a further step involved: to transfer the house into Mrs Blake's name.

All three transactions could be dealt with in a single application to the Land Registry: paying off the mortgage, substituting the names of the executors for Herbert Blake's and substituting Mrs Blake for the executors.

Matthew heard from the building society within a few days, and they told him how much was required to pay off the mortgage. Including a small fee they charged, and allowing for interest up to three months ahead, which they were entitled to claim, the Minford Building Society needed £785·31 to clear the mortgage, and it was for this amount that Matthew sent a cheque to the building society. A week later he received the 'deeds' by registered post: the charge certificate, form 53 bearing the seal of the building society, and a number of old papers relating to the property.

Matthew next prepared the form to transfer the ownership of the house into Mrs Blake's name. He obtained from the Solicitors' Law Stationery Society's Oyez Shop a copy of Land Registry form 56 (Assent or Appropriation). He could have obtained this form from HMSO, the Stationery Office. The document by which personal representatives transfer a house to the person entitled to it under a will or intestacy is usually called an assent, and they are said to assent to the property vesting in the person entitled to it. Form 56 was not difficult to complete. Opposite, is how it read when Matthew had filled in the blanks.

Form 56
HM Land Registry

## ASSENT OR APPROPRIATION

County, county borough
or London borough          *Surrey*
Title number               *SY2121212*
Property        *'The Firs', Willow Lane, Minford*
  (We) *Mary Josephine Blake of 'The Firs', Willow*
         *Lane, Minford, Surrey, widow, and Matthew*
         *John Seaton of 14 Twintree Avenue, Minford,*
         *Surrey, company secretary*
              as personal representative(s) of the late
*Herbert George Blake of 'The Firs', Willow Lane, Min-*
*ford, Surrey, retired factory manager*
hereby assent to the land comprised in the title above
mentioned vesting in: *Mary Josephine Blake*
                        *of 'The Firs', Willow Lane,*
                        *Minford, Surrey*
                        *Widow*
Dated the   7   day of   *September*   *1972*
Signed by the said   *Mary* ⎫
   *Josephine Blake*          ⎬ *M. J. Blake*
                            ⎭
in the presence of
Name:        *David Tench*
Address:   *The Platt, Amersham, Bucks*
Description or
occupation       *author*
Signed by the said   *Matthew* ⎫
                     *John Seaton* ⎬ *M. J. Seaton*
                                  ⎭
in the presence of
Name:        *David Tench*
             *as above*

Form 56 can also be used for a leasehold house, in which case the landlord has to be notified. He may be entitled to receive a copy of the completed form, and to demand a fee.

When form 56 had been completed signed by Mrs Blake and Matthew, and witnessed, Matthew sent it to the appropriate district office of the Land Registry, with a covering letter:

> 14 Twintree Avenue,
> Minford, Surrey.
> 7 September 1972.

Dear Sir,

> *'The Firs', Willow Lane, Minford, Surrey*
> *SY2121212*

I enclose a photocopy of the probate of Herbert George Blake's will, charge certificate for 'The Firs', Willow Lane, forms 53 and 56 and cheque payable to HM Land Registry for £9·50. Please cancel the mortgage and register Mrs Mary Josephine Blake as the new owner.

Please then return the photocopy of the probate and the land certificate to me.

> Yours faithfully,
> Matthew Seaton.

The £9·50 fee was for registering the assent to Mrs Blake, based on the value of the house (there was no fee to pay for cancelling the mortgage). On the back of form 56 was a space to be completed stating the value of the house. This was needed to fix the fee to be paid for registering the transfer of the house to

Mrs Blake. The fee was 50p for every £1,000 of the value of the house (now 45p, with a maximum fee of £225). Matthew completed the 'Statement of Value' and crossed out the reference in the printed part of the form to solicitors. Mrs Blake then signed the form in her capacity of devisee, as the form called her, that is to say the person to whom the property was devised or given by the will. She certified the value of the house as being £19,000, the figure agreed for estate duty purposes, so £9·50 was payable.

Mrs Blake had an acknowledgment from the Land Registry which said how long it would take to deal with the application. Four weeks later she received the land certificate in which Mrs Blake appeared as the registered proprietor. The reference to the mortgage to the Minford Building Society had been crossed out. But there was a note in the land certificate that the property might be liable for more death duties. This was a routine formality and inapt for a case where the estate duty had been paid in full and a clearance certificate issued. At the same time the Land Registry returned the photocopy of the probate. Thus Mrs Blake became registered as the owner of the house in substitution for her late husband, and the mortgage was cleared.

*—unregistered*

If the title to a house is not registered at the Land
Registry, the procedure for transferring the house to
the person entitled to it is likely to be less straight
forward. To find out whether the title is registered or
not, it is necessary to inspect the deeds. If there is no
land certificate with the deeds (or—where there is
a mortgage—no charge certificate), it means that the
title is not registered. A considerable number of areas,
particularly towns and cities, are now covered by a
system of compulsory registration, which means that
the titles to properties there have had to be registered
but only when they are sold. The result is that even in
areas of compulsory registration, some houses
still have unregistered titles. In places where registration
has been compulsory for many years (such as London,
Surrey and Kent) most houses now have registered
titles. Elsewhere it is more likely that the title is not
registered.

In the case of an unregistered title, the executor,
after paying off the mortgage, if there is one, should
find amongst the deeds one deed which is the conveyance of the property to the deceased. (If the house is
leasehold, it is called an assignment.) This is the deed
prepared at the time the house was bought and which
transferred ownership of it to the deceased. This deed
should be used as the basis for preparing the document to transfer ownership to the person now entitled
to it. This document is called an assent, the same
name as is used in the case of a house with a registered title, and in a simple case can be prepared by
the executor himself.

Imagine that Herbert Blake's house had had an

unregistered title, and that the executors had wished to put the house into Mrs Blake's name, now that she was entitled to it. When he had paid off the building society mortgage, Matthew would have received from the building society the title deeds to the house. These would have included the actual mortgage deed, at the back of which would now appear a receipt, bearing the official seal of the building society, which acknowledged that all the money due under the mortgage had now been paid off. The title deeds would also have included the deed of conveyance by which Herbert Blake had become the legal owner of the house at the time of his purchase. Matthew would also have needed the original grant of probate. The assent, on an ordinary sheet of paper, would have read like this:

ASSENT

We hereby assent to the freehold property The Firs, Willow Lane, Minford, Surrey vesting in Mary Josephine Blake (Mrs Blake) of The Firs, Willow Lane, Minford, widow.

We make this assent as executors of the will of Mrs Blake's late husband Herbert George Blake, who died on 12 May 1972.

Probate of his will was granted to us by the Principal Probate Registry on 17 July 1972.

We hereby acknowledge Mrs Blake's right to the production of the probate.

Dated 7 September 1972.

Signed by the executors of the will of Herbert George Blake deceased: Mrs Blake, and Matthew John Seaton of 14 Twintree Avenue, Minford, company secretary.

Signatures: M. J. Seaton     M. J. Blake

Witnesses: David Tench, The Platt, Amersham.

In many cases an assent in that form is sufficient. It should not be used where a mortgage has not yet been paid off, or where there is any complication. In the case of a joint ownership as a rule no assent is needed; a death certificate is sufficient to prove the survivor's title.

This form of assent can be used for a leasehold house, in which case details of the lease should appear in the assent and the landlord should be notified; he may be entitled to a copy of the assent itself and he may demand a fee, depending on the terms of the lease.

An assent is not liable for stamp duty, and does not have to be registered anywhere. It has to be put with the deeds and there it stays. One formality remains, however. There should be written or typed on the back of the original grant of probate a brief memorandum giving the essential details of the assent. In the case of Herbert Blake's house, it would have said something like this:

'Memo: An assent dated 7 September 1972 vested the freehold house The Firs, Willow Lane, Minford, Surrey in Mrs Mary Josephine Blake, and her right to the production of this grant of probate was acknowledged'.

In this way, anyone who buys the property from Mrs Blake is given legal protection, especially against fraud. Mrs Blake as beneficiary is given a specific legal right to be shown at any time the original grant of probate, as she may need to when she comes to sell the house, in which case the grant of probate is one of the documents needed to prove her ownership.

A difficulty in preparing an assent in the case of

unregistered property lies in the fact that there is no one to check it unless and until the property comes to be sold, when the buyer's solicitor will want to look at it. If the executors die before the house comes to be sold and it turns out that the assent was incorrect in some respect, there might be considerable expense and difficulty in putting things right. In the case of registered property, however, the beneficiary knows that the assent is correct as soon as the land certificate, showing him as the new owner, is received back from the land registry.

*Transferring the shares*
The remaining item to be dealt with was the shares. Herbert Blake had owned over £12,000 worth of them. They were shares in large industrial or commercial companies and one local authority holding, all of which were quoted on the London Stock Exchange. The investments were of a kind which, in normal times, Matthew might well have chosen, if asked to advise on the subject. So he suggested that Mrs Blake should take over, as they stood, the investments which her husband had held, and she agreed.

It is sometimes necessary to sell some or all of the shares held by a person who has died, in order to pay the debts, estate duty or the legacies or to meet the expenses of administering the estate. Where this happens, the executors instruct a stockbroker, either directly or through a bank, and all the formalities are dealt with through a broker.

Whether the shares are sold or not, it is necessary for each company in which shares are held to see a copy of the probate. A letter addressed to the registrar of the company at the head office will always ultimately reach the right destination. There is sometimes a fee, varying from 10p to £1, to pay for registering the probate in this way.

Where the shares are to be sold, or where (as in Herbert Blake's case) the shares are to be transferred direct to the beneficiary (the person entitled to have them under the will), it is usually possible to send the probate to the registrar of the company at the same time as sending the transfer of the shares to be dealt with by him.

Matthew intended that the probate be sent to the seven concerns in which shares were held, together with the transfers into Mrs Blake's name of the respective shareholdings. Thus the first thing to be done was to prepare the forms transferring the shares in each case. A separate form would be needed for each transfer; as there were seven transfers Matthew ordered fourteen forms, to be on the safe side. He would prepare each transfer in draft, and then from it write out the actual transfer, although this is not essential, particularly if one is good at filling in forms. He obtained stock transfer forms from the Solicitors' Law Stationery Society's Oyez shop. There are Oyez shops or sales offices in various parts of the country. The London telephone number is 01-407 8055.

The stock transfer form consisted of a number of panels in which the necessary information had to be given. It is a comprehensive document intended to be used for sales, as well as for transfers to beneficiaries following a death, and to be used for all kinds of investments, beside stocks and shares. Government securities and local authority loans, for instance, can be dealt with on the form just as much as stocks and shares in companies. The first panel in the form asked for the 'consideration money'; this means, in the case of a sale of shares, the price at which the shares being transferred were sold. In Matthew's case there was no sale and no price, so he simply wrote 'nil' in that panel. The next panel asked for the 'full name of undertaking'; this means the name of the company, or other organisation, whose shares are being transferred. Matthew wrote here in each of the forms the name of the company concerned, for instance, 'Imperial Chemical Industries Ltd'. The next panel asked for a 'full description of security'. This means the type of stock or shares which are held in the particular company. In three out of the seven cases with which Matthew was dealing he simply wrote 'ordinary stock' in this panel. In the case of the Unilever stock he wrote '8 per cent preference stock', in the case of the Shell shares he wrote 'ordinary 25p shares', and for Norwich Corporation he wrote '5 per cent redeemable stock (1980)'. The appropriate 'full description of security' is found on the stock or share certificate, the document which certifies the ownership of the holding.

The next two panels asked for the number or amount of shares, stock or other security, in words and figures. Here Matthew wrote the quantity of stock or shares. In the case of the ICI stock he wrote 'five hundred and fifty pounds' and '£550'.

The next panel asked for details of the registered holder of the shares. Matthew wrote this: 'Herbert George Blake deceased, late of "The Firs", Willow

Lane, Minford, Surrey. Executors: Mary Josephine Blake and Matthew John Seaton'. In the books of each company, obviously, the stocks and shares were still shown as belonging to Herbert George Blake. The information provided in this panel, coupled with the probate, which would be sent to each company with the transfer, provided the link between what was still registered and the signatures on the bottom of the transfer: Matthew's and Mrs Blake's.

Now came the operative part of the stock transfer form. The panel read as follows: 'I/We hereby transfer the above security out of the name(s) aforesaid to the person(s) named below', and just underneath was the space for Matthew and Mrs Blake to sign in their capacity as Herbert Blake's executors. There were added, in italics, some words which did not apply to this case; these only applied where shares were sold through a stock exchange. Matthew crossed out the words in italics. In the right-hand panel he filled in the date.

Only now came a panel for the particulars of Mrs Blake in her capacity as the person taking over the shares: Full name and full postal address of the person to whom the security is transferred. The form pleaded: 'Please complete in typewriting or in Block Capitals.' This heart-cry was no doubt the result of many transfer forms in the past being completed in illegible writing, to the chagrin of many a company registrar trying to decipher transferees' names and addresses. Matthew simply wrote (in block letters) the necessary information: 'Mrs Mary Josephine Blake, The Firs, Willow Lane, Minford, Surrey'.

In the bottom right-hand corner of the front of the

form was a panel for the 'Stamp or name and address of person lodging this form (if other than the Buying Broker(s))'. Matthew left that blank.

The top half of the back of the form was only to apply to a case where the shares had been divided up into different holdings on a sale, and had no application to Matthew's case, so he left it alone.

The bottom half of the back of the form very much applied to his case, as it dealt with the question of stamp duty. Stamp duty amounting to 1 per cent of the price is paid on the purchase of shares, and after payment the appropriate stamps are embossed on the stock transfer form. Stamp duty which is a percentage of the price is called *ad valorem* duty ('according to the value'). The transfers which Matthew was preparing would not be liable to *ad valorem* stamp duty. They would be liable to stamp duty of 50p each. To be eligible for only 50p stamp duty, a certificate on the form had to be completed to show the circumstances which gave rise to the transfer. There were listed in the form, in paragraphs (a) to (j), the nine main categories where the 50p duty is applicable. It was paragraph (e) which applied to Matthew's situation: 'Transfer to a residuary legatee of stock forming part of the residue divisible under a will'. As Herbert Blake had given the residue of his estate to Mrs Blake, she was the residuary legatee, and the shares formed part of the residue of his estate. There was a space beneath for the signature of the 'transferors', and there Matthew and Mrs Blake both signed.

Sometimes a testator gives a specific legacy of some shares to a named person. ('All my shares in Marks & Spencer to my niece Ann Ogilvy'), as distinct from giving the whole of the residue. The shares given by such a specific legacy would be similarly transferred by a stock transfer form, but in that case the appropriate paragraph to gain the advantage of the 50p stamp duty is (c) instead of (e).

Where shares form part of the estate of someone who died intestate, they may be transferred to the beneficiary by means of a stock transfer form. Exemption from *ad valorem* stamp duty is not always possible then, and depends on complicated technicalities. But where it does apply, paragraph (d) on the back of the stock transfer form is the relevant one.

The next problem was to deal with the payment of the stamp duty on the transfers and to have them sent to the companies concerned, so that Mrs Blake could be registered as the new owner of them. In practice only banks, stockbrokers, solicitors and a few others lodge stock transfers with companies for registration. It is impossible for an ordinary individual to do so without also completing complicated additional declarations. This has to do with exchange control, that is, government measures to prevent money being transferred abroad.

A bank is an obvious choice for this job, and will usually attend to the stamping of the transfers as part of the operation of sending them to the companies concerned. Matthew therefore took the seven transfers of the seven lots of shares, completed, signed and dated, together with photocopies of the probate, to the Minford branch of Barminster Bank, and asked the manager to deal with them. The bank's fee for this was £1 per transfer. The bank also debited the executorship account with the stamp duty of 50p per transfer, and the company registrars' fees.

Banks charge between £1 and £1·50 per transfer, but this fee includes the service of providing and completing the transfer forms. As executors usually have to employ the bank to lodge the transfers for registration, they may as well let the bank do the whole thing, merely sending the stock certificates to the bank manager for the necessary action.

Eventually he received back from the bank the photocopies of the probate together with the new stock or share certificate showing Mrs Blake as the owner. This was her proof of ownership of the shares.

### Letter of request

In a case where the executor is also the person entitled to the shares under the will, no formal transfer of the shares is usually needed. Instead a document called a letter of request (form CON41A published by Oyez) can be used and this is not liable to any stamp duty.

### Distribution according to the will

Little now remained for Matthew to do to complete the administration. having made sure that all expenses and all debts had been paid, he was in a position to make a final distribution. All the expenses involved in the administration of the estate had been paid out of the executors' account at the bank. These expenses included the cost of photocopies of the probate, the stamp duty on the share transfers and the Land

Registry fees relating to the transfer of the house. His own out-of-pocket expenses, on postage and such matters as fares to London to visit the probate registry were refunded out of the executors' bank account, and so were Mrs Blake's expenses as an executor. Personal representatives are not entitled to be paid for the time they devote to the administration of the estate, unless the will specifically says so. But they are not, on the other hand, expected to dip into their own pockets.

Matthew was now in a position to distribute amongst the beneficiaries the rest of the assets, apart from the house, its contents and the shares, which had already been taken over by Mrs Blake. So now he paid the three pecuniary legacies which Herbert Blake had given in his will: £500 to Herbert Blake's daughter Emma, and £750 each to her two brothers, Robert and Mark. Mrs Blake and Matthew signed cheques for these amounts on the executorship account and obtained a receipt from each of the children. Emma's receipt read as follows:

### Herbert George Blake deceased

I acknowledge that I have received the sum of five hundred pounds (£500) from Matthew J. Seaton and Mrs M. J. Blake in settlement of the legacy due to me under the will of my late father, Herbert G. Blake.

Dated: 23 October 1972.
Signed: Emma Seaton.

The will had also provided that Robert should receive the grandfather clock which Herbert Blake inherited from his father. Robert did not yet have a home of his own, and he decided to leave the clock in his mother's home until he was in a position to take it. Nevertheless, it now became his own property. Matthew wrote to him telling him this and obtained from him this acknowledgment:

*Herbert George Blake deceased*

I acknowledge that I have received the grandfather clock left to me by the will of my late father, Herbert G. Blake.

Dated: 26 October 1972
Signed: Robert A. Blake.

Matthew was about to take the conclusive step in the administration, the final distribution of the residue. Personal representatives should consider carefully everything they have done before parting with the remaining asset in their hands.

Matthew went through everything that he had done in connection with the executorship from the moment his father-in-law had died nearly six months before. He looked again at every asset in the estate, he looked at each debt, and at each expense, to see that everything had been done properly. This would have been much more important if several people had been sharing the residue, all the deceased's children, for instance, and it would have been more important still if there had been any dissent within the family. Reviewing all his actions over the previous months, Matthew found everything to be in order. Thus the executors were in a position to make the final payment to Mrs Blake, and this cleared the executorship bank account, which they then closed.

Matthew went through the details of the administration with Mrs Blake, showing her exactly what had been done. He prepared, and they both signed, accounts showing how the final payment which she received was arrived at, taking into account all the receipts and payments that had been through their hands. It was not necessary that these accounts should take any particular form. They merely showed a list of the assets, distinguished between those which Mrs Blake had taken over in kind (the house, the contents of the house, the car, and the shares), and those which had been converted into money. It showed the debts, the funeral expenses, and the administration expenses, and then showed a balance in hand. The legacies, amounting to £2,000, were set out in the account and the net balance was the amount which she had received.

In this way the administration by the executors was brought to an end. Matthew bundled all the papers together, including the original probate, and put them in a large envelope. This he placed in the drawer where he had found the deed-box with his father-in-law's will, the day after he had died. There the papers would stay. Mrs Blake sought his advice about what she should do with the cash she now had in her bank account, about her newly acquired shareholdings, about transferring into her own name the insurance on what she had inherited, about what to do with the car, and about similar matters, but in doing these things she was consulting him as her son-in-law, and not as an executor. The administration of the estate was over.

Administration in Scotland

*The process which in England is called proving the will or obtaining probate is in Scotland referred to as obtaining (or expeding) confirmation. Confirmation is the decree of a competent court declaring and confirming that certain persons are entitled, as executors, to administer and wind up the estate of the deceased, as specified in an inventory given to the court. If the executors have been named in a will left by the deceased, they are commonly referred to as executors-nominate. If they are not so named (for example in the case of intestacy) they are commonly referred to as executors-dative.*

*The process of expeding confirmation in Scotland follows much the same pattern as the process of obtaining probate in England: the investigation and valuation of the estate, the preparation of an inventory and the assessing of estate duty differ very little from what has been described above. The actual application for confirmation is dealt with below. After obtaining confirmation, the executors would exhibit it to the various persons who require to see it, collect all the estate together, pay out all debts and legacies and wind up the estate according to the deceased's wishes (if he left a will) or according to the rules of intestacy (if he did not).*

*The courts which deal with applications for confirmation in Scotland are the sheriff courts. When they deal with such matters, the sheriff courts are technically known as commissary courts. Commissary business is conducted on the basis of sherrifdom.*

*Apart from small estates under £1,000 in net value and under £3,000 in gross value, there is no proce-*

dure laid down in Scotland similar to the personal application procedure already described for english cases. It is always open to the executor to apply to the court personally for confirmation, but no special facilities exist to guide the personal applicant through the various formalities which have to be observed. He might find it difficult to make his own way unaided.

In the case of an intestacy, the first step is to apply to the court within whose jurisdiction the deceased has died and to ask that court to appoint some person to the office of executor. Generally this would be one or more of the relatives entitled to succeed to the deceased's estate under the rules of intestacy. The application is made by means of what is called an initial writ. If there is no competition for the office of executor, the sheriff will in due course grant a decree pronouncing the applicant to be the executor-dative of the deceased. The executors so appointed will have to provide some security for the due performance of their office.

Executors (whether they be nominate or dative) are responsible for the preparation of an inventory of the estate of the deceased in much the same way as in England. The inventory has to be sworn ('deponed to' is the scottish expression) by one of the executors before a notary public (who fulfils much the same function as does a commissioner for oaths in England) or a justice of the peace. The inventory is then signed by the executor and by the notary public.

This inventory serves a dual purpose. In the first place, it is on the basis of this inventory that the estate duty is assessed by the Inland Revenue. Accordingly, there is attached a long list of questions *(much the same questions as Matthew Seaton had to answer), enquiring into the details of the deceased's estate. The executor must answer these and depone that all his answers are true to the best of his knowledge and belief. Once this has been done, the estate duty payable is provisionally assessed by the Inland Revenue and paid.*

*Thereafter the same inventory is lodged with the local commissary court and the court is asked to confirm that the executors who have sworn the inventory are the persons entitled to uplift and administer the various items of estate listed in the inventory. The act of confirmation (or confirmation) as the decree of the court is called, therefore contains a complete list of those items of estate to which the executors have a title. This is different from what happens in England, where the probate of the will does not specify the various items of estate to which the executors have a title. And there is one other consequence arising from this difference in procedure: if there has been some item of estate missed out from the original inventory, the executors have to give a corrective inventory listing this additional estate, not only to the Inland Revenue but also to the court. The court then issues what is called an 'eik' to the confirmation, confirming the executors' title to this additional estate.*

*To assist the executors to gather in the estate the court will, if asked, issue in addition to the confirmation itself, certificates of confirmation for any item of estate. Each certificate is, as it were, an extract from the confirmation itself, and is limited to one particular part of the estate. This certificate can then be exhibited to the person concerned in relation to that* particular item of estate, and this is sufficient to prove the executor's title.

For small estates, where the gross value is not more than £3,000 and the net value is not more than £1,000 a special procedure is available. The application for confirmation may be made personally to the local sheriff clerk. The clerk will prepare and fill up the inventory, oath and revenue statement (form B3) from information supplied by the applicant. Even in the case of an intestacy, no initial writ is required. But if the applicant is applying by virtue of his kinship, then proof of his kinship is required. This proof may be supplied by the oath of two witnesses who should attend with the applicant. If security is required, the cautioner who provides it usually attends with the applicant and signs the bond. The inventory is deponed to and recorded and confirmation is expede and delivered to the applicant on payment of a small fee.

The confirmation is the executors' title to the moveable property and heritable property of the deceased. Moreover, the confirmation may in the case of a house be used as the basis of a transfer by the executors to the persons entitled to it whether in satisfaction of their legal rights, under the rules of intestacy, or by the deceased's will. The executors can effect the transfer merely by endorsing a short docquet on the confirmation as follows:

We, Madeleine Jean Burns and Michael James Scott being by virtue of the within confirmation the executors on the estate of the deceased Hugh Geoffrey Burns so far as specified in the confirmation hereby nominate Madeleine Jean Burns as the person entitled in part implement of the will of the said Hugh Geoffrey Burns to the following item of estate that is to say the dwelling-house known as The Pines, Birch Lane, Edinburgh being number 5 of the items of the estate specified in the said confirmation.

The procedure adopted by personal representatives is broadly the same whether they are executors (appointed in a will) who apply for a grant of probate, or administrators (on an intestacy) who apply for a grant of letters of administration. But when it comes to distributing the estate, executors follow the wishes of the deceased according to the will. Administrators must apply the intestacy rules laid down in the Administration of Estates Act.

The nearest next-of-kin should apply for the grant. The widow, or widower, is primarily entitled to be the administrator. If there is no surviving spouse, or if he or she does not apply for a grant, then any of the children may apply. Grandchildren may apply, if their parents are dead. Next, the deceased's parents may apply, and then brothers and sisters, or their children. They are followed by half-brothers and half-sisters, or their children. Next grandparents, followed by uncles and aunts (or their children) may apply, finishing up with uncles and aunts of the half blood, or their children. No relations remoter than those are legally next-of-kin so as to be entitled to apply for a grant of letters of administration. Normally it is not necessary to have more than one administrator, but where someone under 18 is entitled to the estate, or part of it, or where a life interest arises under the intestacy rules, there must be at least two administrators.

The division of the net estate where a person died without leaving a will depends on the value of what is left, and what family survives. The net estate is what remains of the estate after paying the debts, the funeral expenses, the estate duty, the expenses of getting the letters of administration, and of administering the estate. Here are some examples.

## Where the deceased left a wife or husband

EXAMPLE A

Deceased's family: wife and three children

Net estate: personal effects (that is, car, furniture, clothing, jewellery and all goods and chattels) and £9,500 (in Savings Bank, savings certificates, house)

Division of estate under intestacy rules:

all to wife

Explanation: As the net estate, apart from the personal effects, is less than £15,000, everything goes to the surviving spouse, and the children get nothing. No other relatives (for example, parents) are entitled to any part of the estate. It would be the same in the case of a wife dying intestate.

EXAMPLE B

Deceased's family: wife and four children

Net estate: personal effects, and £17,000 in investments and value of house

Division of estate under intestacy rules:

(1) wife gets:

(a) personal effects

(b) £15,000 plus interest on it at 4 per cent per annum from date of death till payment

(c) a life interest in £1,000 (that is, the income from £1,000 for the rest of her life)

(2) each of four children gets:

(a) £250 immediately

(b) £250 on mother's death

Explanation: The intestacy rules give the widow all the personal effects, £15,000 (plus interest at 4 per cent from the date of death to the date of payment) and a life interest in half the remainder. The children share the second half of the remainder immediately, and the first half on their mother's death. If one of the children had died before the father, leaving any children, then those grandchildren of the deceased would have shared their parent's proportion of their grandfather's estate. It makes no difference if the widow is not the mother of some or all of the children; where, for instance, their father married a second time, the estate is shared as described between the widow and the deceased's children, both her children by him and her stepchildren. Any children or grandchildren under age do not inherit until coming of age or getting married. Other relatives (parents, or step-children, of the deceased, for instance) get nothing.

EXAMPLE C

Deceased's family: husband, mother, no children

Net estate:          personal effects, £25,000 in investments

Division of estate under intestacy rules:

                    all to husband

Explanation:        Where there are no children, the surviving husband or wife takes all the personal effects, plus everything else up to £40,000. Mother gets nothing.

EXAMPLE D

Deceased's family: wife, mother and father, two brothers, no children

Net estate:          personal effects, plus £47,000 in investments and house

Division of estate under intestacy rules:

                    (1) wife gets:
                    (a) personal effects
                    (b) £40,000, plus interest on it at 4 per cent per annum from date of death until payment
                    (c) £3,500
                    (2) mother gets £1,750
                    (3) father gets £1,750

Explanation:        The surviving wife or husband takes the personal effects and £40,000, plus interest until payment. The rest is divided in two; the surviving spouse takes one half, and the other half is divided equally between the deceased's parents (the brothers get nothing). If there had been only one parent alive, he or she would have received the whole of the parents' £3,500. If he had no parents living, his brothers would share equally that £3,500; the share of any brother or sister who died before the deceased would be divided equally between his or her children.

EXAMPLE E

Deceased's family: husband, no children, no parents, no brothers or sisters, no nephews or nieces, no grandparents; one aunt, four cousins.

Net estate: personal effects, £140,000 in investments

Division of estate under intestacy rules:
all to husband

Explanation: If, apart from the surviving spouse, the nearest relations are aunts, uncles, cousins, or grandparents (that is, no children, parents or siblings, nephews or nieces), the surviving spouse takes everything, no matter how much it is.

**Where the deceased left no wife or husband**

EXAMPLE F

Deceased's family: no wife, three children, seven grandchildren, two of whom are children of a son who died some years before

Net estate: £4,000 including personal effects

Division of estate under intestacy rules:

(1) each of the three surviving children gets £1,000 (× 3 = £3,000)

(2) each of the two grandchildren whose father died before the deceased gets £500 (× 2 = £1,000)

(3) the other grandhildren get nothing

Explanation: Where there is no wife or husband, the whole estate is shared between the children equally. It makes no difference how big or small the estate is. The share of any child who has already died is shared equally between his children; this process of taking a deceased parent's share can go on to the third and fourth generation, if necessary. Any children or grandchildren who are under age do not get a share until they come of age, or marry.

EXAMPLE G

Deceased's family: two brothers

Net estate:          £3,000 including personal effects

Division of estate under intestacy rules:

                     £1,500 to each brother

Explanation:         If the parents of a bachelor or a spinster (or widow or widower without descendants) are both dead, the whole estate is shared between brothers and sisters equally. The share of a deceased brother or sister goes to his or her children. If there had been a parent alive, he or she would have taken everything, and brothers and sisters would have received nothing. If both parents are alive, they share the estate equally.

                     Relatives of the whole blood take priority over relatives of the half blood. If, for example a bachelor whose parents are dead has one brother and one half-brother, the brother takes everything and the half-brother takes nothing. But if there is no brother of the whole blood, then a half-brother would take everything in priority to grandparents, or aunts, uncles or cousins. The same applies to other relatives of the half blood: they only take if corresponding relatives of the whole blood (or

their descendants) are not alive to
inherit a share. An illegitimate
child or an adopted child counts
as being a child of the full blood
for the purpose of inheritance.

EXAMPLE H

Deceased's family: one aunt, two uncles, three
cousins who are children of a
deceased uncle, four cousins who
are children of a deceased aunt,
five cousins who are children of
the two living uncles; no children,
no parents, no brothers or sisters,
no grandparents

Net estate: £6,000

Division of estate under intestacy rules:

(1) £1,200 each to the aunt and
two uncles (×3 = £3,600)

(2) £400 each to the three
cousins who are children of a
deceased uncle (×3 = £1,200)

(3) £300 each to the four cousins
who are children of a deceased
aunt (×4 = £1,200)

Explanation: The aunts and uncles, being the
nearest relatives, share the estate
equally. But children of any dead
aunt or dead uncle share what that
aunt or uncle would have received
if he or she had survived long
enough. So the estate is divided
into five; the one-fifth share of the

dead uncle is divided into three equal shares for his children, the three cousins on that side of the family, and the one-fifth share of the dead aunt is divided into four equal shares for her children, the four cousins on that side of the family. The cousins whose relevant parent is still alive get nothing.

EXAMPLE J

Deceased's family: five second cousins (relatives who have the same great-grandparents as the deceased)

Net estate: £10,000.

Division of estate under intestacy rules:

everything to the crown.

Explanation: Only relatives who can show that they are descendants of (or are) the deceased's grandparents can take a share in the estate of someone who died intestate. To be a descendant of the deceased's great-grandparent is not sufficient, and if there are no nearer relatives, the estate goes to the crown. It is then called *bona vacantia*, property to which no one can claim a title. Often the Treasury Solicitor, who administers *bona vacantia*, makes a distribution of some or even all of the net estate, after paying the expenses, amongst those who can show a strong moral claim: where a distant relative has looked after the deceased for many years, for example, or where a void will has been made which would have left everything to a close friend. This may also happen where the deceased had been living with a woman to whom he was not married.

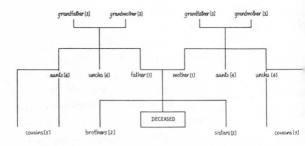

*who inherits the property of a bachelor who died intestate*

## In Scotland

*Under the Succession (Scotland) Act 1964 (which applies to the estate of persons whose domicile was in Scotland when they died) a widow or widower has, on intestacy, certain prior rights in the estate of the spouse who has died. These prior rights are, briefly, as follows:*

—*the right to the deceased's interest in the house up to the value of £15,000 in which the surviving spouse was ordinarily resident. Where the value of the house is in excess of £15,000, the surviving spouse is entitled to the sum of £15,000 in place of the house;*

—*the right to the furniture and plenishing of the house up to the value of £5,000;*

—*the sum of £2,500 if there are children, grandchildren or great-grandchildren of the deceased, or the sum of £5,000 if there are no children or other issue.*

*In other words, the prior rights of the surviving spouse will in the vast majority of cases account for the house and furniture and also the first £2,500 (or £5,000) beyond these.*

*After prior rights the legal rights already referred to have to be calculated. The balance then remaining is distributed as follows:*

*(1) Amongst the descendants of the deceased: the children (including adopted and illegitimate children), but if there are none then grandchildren, then great-grandchildren and so on. The children of any child who has predeceased will come in for the parent's share.*

*(2) Failing descendants (a) one half goes to the father and mother of the deceased in equal shares (or to the survivor if there is only one*

*parent then alive); and (b) the other half goes
to the collateral line: brothers and sisters, but
if there are none then nephews and nieces, or
then grand-nephews and grand-nieces and so
on. Half-brothers and sisters and their family
only succeed if there are no brothers or sisters
of the full blood. If neither the father nor the
mother of the deceased survive, the collateral
line takes everything.*

(3) *Failing collaterals and their descendants,
everything goes to the father and mother of the
deceased equally or, if one has predeceased, to
the survivor.*

(4) *Failing the father and mother, everything goes
to the surviving widower or widow of the
deceased.*

(5) *Failing a surviving spouse, everything goes to
uncles and aunts and if they are dead then to
their descendant line. Uncles and aunts of the
half blood only succeed if there are no surviving uncles and aunts of the full blood.*

(6) *Failing uncles and aunts, everything goes to
the grandparents of the deceased.*

(7) *Failing grandparents, everything goes to great-
uncles and great-aunts or to their descendant
line. Again relatives of the full blood take
preference over those of the half blood.*

(8) *Failing great-uncles and great-aunts, everything goes to the great-grandparents of the deceased, failing whom, their collateral line.*

*If there is no one to succeed as above then the crown
will take the estate.*

Acknowledging signature, 44
administration, 48, 50, 55, 60, 138, 139
— costs, 10, 12, 53
— letters of, 48, 50, 58, 112, 145
administrators, 48, 58, 112, 145
adopted child, 7, 93, 155
ad valorem, 133, 134
affirmation, 112
assent, 122, 123, 124, 127, 128, 129
attestation clause, 34, 35, 44
aunts, 2, 7, 145, 152, 156

bachelor, 2, 151, 154
bank, 1, 21, 22, 42, 51, 59, 62, 71, 87, 88, 97, 110, 115, 116, 118, 134, 138
— as executor, 12, 13
bequests, 22, 24, 51
— specific, 6, 7, 9, 10, 14, 22, 24
birth certificate, 38
bona vacantia, 153
brothers, 2, 6, 30, 52, 145, 151
— half, 145, 151
building society, 21, 22, 26, 68, 69, 90, 119, 120, 125, 127
burial or cremation, 17, 22, 24, 31, 56
business, 5, 105

capital, 3
car, 1, 22, 48, 59, 81, 99, 138
charging clause, 12
clearance certificate, 118, 119, 125
codicil, 41, 55
confirmation, 140 *et seq*
corrective affidavit, 119
cousins, 152, 153
creditors (advertising for), 85, 86
crown (property going to), 1, 2, 153, 156

death
— certificates, 49, 50, 77, 91, 106, 128
— grant, 78, 79, 115
— simultaneous, 3, 14, 15, 16, 24, 27, 30, 57
debts, 6, 51, 52, 53, 56, 84 *et seq*, 101, 104, 105, 106, 116, 119, 135, 138, 140, 145
Department of Health and Social Security, 77, 115
discretionary payment, 77
disinheriting, 46
distribution, 135, 137
district valuer, 65, 67, 118
divorce, 2, 43
domicile, 1

endowment policy, 21, 22
engrossment, 23
Ernie, 62
estate, 3
— duty, 5, 9, 10, 16, 51, 53, 66, 76, 77, 79, 101, 103, 106 *et seq*, 115, 118, 125, 141, 145
— (additional), 118
— money for, 87 *et seq*
executors, 4, 9, 10 *et seq*, 15, 22, 24, 26, 30, 31, 38, 39, 48, 55, 57, 58, 63, 87, 88, 89, 112, 125, 126, 127, 129, 139, 142, 144, 145
— as trustees, 24, 25, 26, 27, 28, 29, 31, 32, 36, 55, 56
— dative, 140, 141
— nominate, 140, 141
— substitute, 13, 32

freehold, 99, 127
free of duty, 10
funeral expenses, 10, 25, 31, 55, 56, 85, 91, 105, 106, 138, 145
furniture, 1, 22, 48, 61, 83

gifts (and estate duty), 102, 103
Giro, 13, 50, 62, 89
grandchildren, 7, 28, 29, 32, 36, 145, 147, 150, 155
grandparents, 2, 145, 149, 151, 152, 153, 156
grant of probate, 48, 49, 50, 51, 54, 58, 63, 87, 88, 91, 108, 112, 113, 127, 128
guarantee, 112, 113
guardian, 17

heritable property, 47
hire purchase, 83, 85, 104, 116
holograph, 45
house, 1, 21, 22, 25, 29, 32, 47, 48, 65 *et seq*, 81, 99, 100, 101, 102, 117, 118, 136, 138
– transfer of, 119 *et seq*

initial writ, 141
Inland Revenue, 5, 65, 99, 141
insurance, 1, 39, 51, 57, 59, 64, 88, 90, 98, 103, 113, 115
– house, 120, 139
intestacy
– partial, 14
– rules, 1, 2, 3, 15, 141, 143, 145, 155
intestate, 1, 2, 46, 47, 48, 134, 145
inventory, 141, 142
investment, 3, 20, 25, 26, 27, 29, 32, 70, 95

joint account, 63, 64, 90, 104
joint property, 16, 62, 64, 65, 66, 67, 68, 104, 105, 128

land certificate, 121, 125, 129
Land Registry, 121, 123, 124, 125, 129, 136
– forms, 121, 122
leasehold, 99, 100, 124, 126, 128

legacy, 14, 22, 24, 51, 53, 57, 133
– losing, 33
– pecuniary, 10, 40
legal rights, 46, 47, 143
letter of request, 135
life interest, 1, 3, 12, 20, 30, 52, 145

marriage certificate, 38, 49, 78
minority interests, 52
mortgage, 6, 21, 22, 59, 67, 68, 90, 101, 105, 119, 120, 121, 124, 125, 127, 128
moveable estate, 46, 47

National savings, 49, 50, 59, 60, 61, 90, 95, 115, 116
– certificate, 38, 39, 57, 59, 61, 89, 90, 94, 103, 116
nephews, 7, 156
nieces, 156
nominating property, 49, 62, 103

oath, 54, 94, 144

parents, 2, 145, 155
– death, 25, 29, 32, 145
– share, 2, 25, 32, 155
pension, 49, 74 *et seq*, 90, 91, 99, 104
– retirement, 77, 78, 115
– scheme, 21, 74, 75, 76, 77, 80, 90, 91, 99, 104, 115
– widow's, 74, 75, 76, 77, 78, 79, 91, 104
personal application, 106, 108, 111, 141
– forms for, 86, 91 *et seq*, 106, 111
personal effects, 1, 48, 52
personal representative, 48, 50, 53, 85, 110, 111, 112, 113, 119, 136, 138, 145
premium bonds, 50, 61, 89, 95
prior rights, 47

probate, 48, 78, 85, 89, 112, 113, 114, 116, 139
– fees, 53, 54, 59, 87, 92, 106, 108, 109, 110, 115
– registering of, 116, 130
– registry, 51, 86, 87, 89, 91, 93, 106, 108, 111, 112, 113
proving the will, 34, 58
public trustee, 13

quick succession relief, 16

registered property, 121 *et seq*
revocation of nomination, 50
revocation of will, 20, 21, 22, 24, 30, 31, 37, 41, 42, 43, 46, 55
– by marriage, 42, 43, 46
residuary legatee, 10, 53, 133,
– dying first, 14
residue, 8, 10, 14, 16, 23, 51, 53, 56, 133, 138
reversion, 20

savings bank, 49, 50, 57, 59, 61, 89, 90, 97, 103, 116
settlement, 102
sisters, 2, 6, 52, 145, 151
solicitor, 5, 6, 11, 51, 52, 53, 54, 55, 108, 125, 129
– as executor, 4, 11
spinster, 2
stamp duty, 38, 128, 133, 135
stock exchange, 21, 70, 74, 96, 129
– Official List, 71, 72, 94, 96
stocks and shares, 1, 5, 21, 22, 26, 48, 70 *et seq*, 95 *et seq*

– certificate, 39, 57, 70
– transfer of, 125 *et seq*, 138

tenant (in common), 66, 67
– joint, 16, 66, 67
testing clause, 44
title deeds, 38, 39, 68, 120, 121, 122
trust, 3, 5, 12, 15, 18, 20, 24 *et seq*, 31, 32, 51
– declaration of, 68
trustee securities, 26

uncles, 2, 7, 145, 152, 156
unit trusts, 73, 95
unregistered property, 126 *et seq*

value (total), 1, 59, 82, 97
valuer, 65, 67, 118

widow (all going to), 1, 2, 107, 110
widow's death, 1
wife, 30, 31
wife's death, 2, 14 *et seq*, 19, 20, 57
will, 1 *et seq*
– alteration to, 23, 40, 41 (in Scotland), 45
– cutting out of, 5, 9
– dating, 33
– form, 4, 5, 45, 52
– registering, 37
– signing, 4, 23, 25, 29, 33 *et seq* (in Scotland), 44
– witnessing, 4, 23, 33 *et seq* (in Scotland), 44, 45

**What to do when someone dies**
deals with the procedures that follow a death. It covers such
formalities as doctors' certificates; reporting a death to the
coroner and what this entails; registration of a death and the
various certificates involved. Burial and cremation are discussed and the arrangements necessary for a funeral. A final
section deals with national insurance benefits that can be
claimed by dependants.

The Consumer Publication *What to do when someone dies*
is complementary to *Wills and probate*.

**The legal side of buying a house**
explains the legal processes of buying an owner-occupied
house with a registered title in England or Wales (not Scotland) and describes the part played by the solicitors, the
building society, the estate agent, surveyor, Land Registry,
insurance company and local authority. It takes you step by
step through a typical purchase and also deals with the legal
side of selling a house.

**Claiming on home, car and holiday insurance**
explains the procedure for making a claim on an insurance
policy, interpreting the technical jargon and identifying the
people and problems you may come across.

**How to sue in the county court**
goes step by step through what is involved in taking a case to
the county court without a solicitor. A woman who sues the
shop that sold her a faulty washing machine is used as an
example to explain the procedure and rules.

**Extending your house**
explains what has to be done, when and by whom, when you
are having an extension built on. It deals with sketch plans,
professional advice, planning permission, building regula-
tions, builders, contracts, and construction.

**Coping with disablement**
gives advice and information to help someone disabled by
increasing age or an accident or illness to lead as independent
a life as possible about the house and outside. Many aids and
techniques for dressing and carrying out everyday tasks are
described, and sources of help—local authority, the health
service, voluntary bodies—are given.

**Getting a divorce**
explains the procedure for getting a divorce in England and
Wales, discusses the grounds for divorce, legal advice and
legal aid, the hearing, costs, and arrangements for children
and finances afterwards.

**Infertility**
sets out what can and should happen in the systematic
investigation of childlessness, explaining the medical and
surgical treatment available.

**How to adopt**
describes the process of adoption, discussing eligibility to
adopt, the legal position, and the effect of an adoption order.

**Pregnancy month by month**
goes in detail through what should happen during pregnancy,
mentioning some of the things that could go wrong and what
can be done about them, and describing the available welfare
services.

**The newborn baby**
deals primarily with the first weeks after the baby is born, with information about feeding and development in the following weeks and months. There is advice about when to seek help from midwife, health visitor, clinic doctor or general practitioner.

**Health for old age**
sets out in plain language the minor and major physical changes that arise as people grow older, and the treatments available to relieve them. Advice is given about maintaining health and about going to the doctor.

**Arrangements for old age**
describes services and organisations available to help older people, and discusses occupation, the state pension, health, living at home or in a residential home.

**Having an operation**
describes the procedure on admission to hospital: ward routine, hospital personnel, preparation for the operation, anaesthesia, post-operative treatment, convalescence. basic information is given about some of the more common operations.

**Treatment and care in mental illness**
deals briefly with the illnesses concerned and describes the help available from the local authority and voluntary organisations. It explains the medical treatment a mentally ill person receives as an outpatient or an inpatient, and deals with community care and aftercare.

**Caring for teeth**
tells people how to look after their teeth, giving advice about oral hygiene, the general dental service, private dentistry, dental diseases, false teeth, and what to do in an emergency.

**Eyes right**
explains how the eyes work, and describes in detail various
eye diseases and complaints, giving advice on seeking treatment through the NHS or privately.

**Care of the feet**
discusses the structure and growth of the feet and how to look
after them, including choosing suitable shoes. Various foot
troubles and deformities, and the treatments available from
doctor or chiropodist to relieve them, are explained.

**Electricity supply and safety**
explains in simple terms what everyone should know about
the electricity supply in the home and how to use many
everyday appliances safely and sensibly. It also deals with
paying for electricity.

**Owning a car**
written for the ignorant car owner-driver, explains what is
involved in buying a car (new or second-hand), running,
repairing and maintaining it, and what can be done when it
breaks down.

**Central heating**
discusses the factors to consider when having central heating
installed: choosing the fuel, the method of insulation, suitable
temperatures, and it helps you to find a good installer. The
book describes, explains and illustrates the various types of
boiler, radiators, convectors, circulation systems and
methods of control. It gives advice on avoiding hazards and
on dealing with problems after the installation.

**Consumer Publications** are available from Consumers' Association, Caxton Hll, Hertford SG 13 7LZ and from booksellers.